"When my friend Steve Berger talks about heaven, I sit up and listen. I've walked with Steve as he's faced the trials of this life, and I've observed how he has emerged with a deeper faith and love for the Father and the people around him. What he has taught me makes me long for heaven. It also makes me want to spend my time on earth making a difference . . . and finishing well."

—Michael W. Smith

"Sometimes we feel stuck—stuck between the hope of heaven and the pain of this world. In *Between Heaven and Earth*, my friend Steve Berger shows us how to not only live in that tension, but how—and why—we should embrace it."

—Dave Ramsey, *New York Times* bestselling author
and nationally syndicated radio show host

"A beloved pastor and teacher, Steve Berger taught for years on the reality of heaven even as we serve Christ on earth, never knowing that one tragic event would bring both realities irrevocably into sharp focus in a moment. Steve discovered that some of God's most precious gifts come in boxes that make our hands bleed when we open them. Few know that at the depth he has experienced. Some of God's greatest mysteries are wrapped up in tragedy, but the tear-stained wisdom mined in that darkness is a gift to us all. In this marvelous book, heaven will become a greater reality even as we are invited to live our lives on earth with greater passion."

—Sheila Walsh, author of *The Storm Inside*

"I grew up hearing people say, 'Some Christians are so heavenly minded they are of no earthly good.' Nowadays it seems like the church has become so earthly minded we're of no heavenly

good. In *Between Heaven and Earth*, my friend Pastor Steve Berger shows us the absolute necessity of having a heavenly mind-set (Colossians 3:1–2) in order to make a real difference in people's lives while we remain on earth. Embrace the truths of this book—learn how to have your heart in heaven and your hand in the harvest. It's one decision you'll never regret!"

—Jeremy Camp

"I'm very grateful to be one of Steve's 'sheep' at Grace Chapel in Tennessee; his teaching consistently gives me a clearer picture of our Creator Redeemer and how we're called to live as Christ-followers. And much like the way his sermons keep me leaning forward on Sunday mornings, this new book, *Between Heaven and Earth*, captured my attention from the start. The bottom line is Steve has a rich, compelling perspective on Glory that will give you fresh grace to lean in to the perfect love of Jesus today. Therefore, I encourage readers not to stop at just one—instead buy a whole case of these puppies and pass them out to all your friends and family!"

—Lisa Harper, author, Bible teacher,
and Women of Faith speaker

"In stark contrast to the Bible—and the whole of Christian history—today's believers think little about heaven and much about the comforts, challenges, and distractions of this life. In this much-needed corrective, Pastor Steve Berger challenges and equips us to be more heavenly minded, so we can, in fact, be more earthly good."

—Michael Hyatt, *New York Times* bestselling author

BETWEEN
HEAVEN
AND EARTH

BETWEEN HEAVEN
AND EARTH

Finding Hope, Courage,
and Passion Through a Fresh
Vision of Heaven

STEVE BERGER

BETHANY HOUSE PUBLISHERS
a division of Baker Publishing Group
Minneapolis, Minnesota

Published by Bethany House Publishers
11400 Hampshire Avenue South
Bloomington, Minnesota 55438
www.bethanyhouse.com

Bethany House Publishers is a division of
Baker Publishing Group, Grand Rapids, Michigan

Printed in the United States of America

Library of Congress Cataloging-in-Publication Data
Berger, Steve.
    Between heaven and earth : finding hope, courage, and passion through a fresh vision of heaven / Steve Berger.
        pages cm
    Includes bibliographical references.
    Summary: "Pastor Steve Berger describes and explains what he's learned about heaven since his teenaged son's tragic death—and applies it to the here and now"—Provided by publisher.
    ISBN 978-0-7642-1167-6 (pbk. : alk. paper)
    1. Heaven—Christianity. I. Title.
BT846.3.B437 2014
236'.24—dc23   2013039242

Unless otherwise indicated, Scripture quotations are from the New King James Version. Copyright © 1982 by Thomas Nelson, Inc. Used by permission. All rights reserved.

Scripture quotations identified AMP are from the Amplified® Bible, copyright © 1954, 1958, 1962, 1964, 1965, 1987 by The Lockman Foundation. Used by permission.

Scripture quotations identified NLT are from the Holy Bible, New Living Translation, copyright © 1996, 2004, 2007 by Tyndale House Foundation. Used by permission of Tyndale House Publishers, Inc., Carol Stream, Illinois 60188. All rights reserved.

Scripture quotations identified RSV are from the Revised Standard Version of the Bible, copyright 1952 [2nd edition, 1971] by the Division of Christian Education of the National Council of the Churches of Christ in the United States of America. Used by permission. All rights reserved.

Cover design by Levan Fisher Design

Author is represented by Wolgemuth & Associates.

14   15   16   17   18   19   20   7   6   5   4   3   2   1

In keeping with biblical principles of creation stewardship, Baker Publishing Group advocates the responsible use of our natural resources. As a member of the Green Press Initiative, our company uses recycled paper when possible. The text paper of this book is composed in part of post-consumer waste.

green
press
INITIATIVE

Sarah Berger is one remarkable woman. She is beautiful inside and out. She is as courageous a person as I've ever met. She is the epitome of a Proverbs 31 woman of God. I married beyond myself—by a long shot. I am eternally grateful for the unspeakable privilege of being her husband. I dedicate this book to you, my beloved Sarah.

My children, all four of them—Heather, Josiah, Cody, and Destiny—are the apples of my eye. When a young parent hopes and prays and then hopes and prays some more that his children will grow up to love Jesus and be faithful to Him, and then that prayer gets answered, it is the greatest joy a parent can have. I have that joy! Thank you, precious ones, for the honor of being your dad. I dedicate this book to all of you.

Finally, to all who know the tension between being a faithful servant while remaining here on earth, and the ache of anxiously waiting for the appearing of our great God and Savior Jesus Christ and the revealing of His glorious heavenly Kingdom, this book is dedicated to you. Keep your heart in heaven and your hand in the harvest.

Foreword

All of us live in a kind of half-world—suspended between this earth, which is so real to us, and heaven, which is so hard to imagine. Only those who have trudged on through unspeakable pain to gain a grander, holier sight of that Beyond can write as Steve Berger does. His is a real voice. Nothing phony. No platitudes. Reality. Terrible, wonderful, powerful reality. Reality is apparent in every line of this book. Yet Berger's is not a voice simply marinating in self-pity. His is the voice of a victor, not a victim.

Among the most trite and irritating accusations hurled at Christians by secular accusers is that they are "so heavenly minded as to be no earthly good." Berger answers those accusations by showing us that seeing over the wall into heaven actually makes us of more earthly good. The tragedy that befell the Bergers not only changed their view of death and heaven, but their entire approach to life and mission. They emerged victorious and dedicated, not just with heaven on their minds, but also with a renewed commitment to souls and lives here and now.

Their victory came out of terrible, heart-wrenching trial. There are those horrible moments—not many, thank God—in which everything seems to stand still and every pain-filled second lasts an eternity. When those seasons come, and they do to every life, time draws out like a blade. Pain, like the night, engulfs us, but we know we cannot just stop hurting. We must wade through the murky darkness as grief washes over us in waves. It's there at the rugged face of that *apparently* oh so solid, impenetrable wall of final separation that we long for a view, just a glance at the other side. We ache to see the afterward of our loved ones. If we could just see what they are experiencing, just know beyond a shadow of a doubt that they are . . . what? Safe, I suppose. Or perhaps happy or joyful or just alive.

Those who grieve without faith cannot hope to see over the wall. Faith is our stepladder that we may scale to get a peek, but just a peek, over it. Blessed are the writers who help us see over to the other side and show us how to rejoice even in our unimaginable suffering.

Every parent's nightmare is to bury a child. It is not the way things ought to be. It is different from every other grief because it is so horribly out of order. The Bergers went through that nightmare, and no attempt is made to hide the pain. Yet when you read the last page and close this book, I believe you will feel, as I did, a contradiction of emotions. I was sorry the Bergers passed through their hall of pain, but I was glad of the book it produced through them.

Here, then, is *Between Heaven and Earth*. Climb up, peek over the wall. Be healed, be inspired, and find the joy unspeakable of having your heart's eyes focused on heaven while having your hand faithfully working in the harvest.

—Dr. Mark Rutland
president, Oral Roberts University

Acknowledgments

My friend Wayne Hastings is an invaluable part of my life and ministry as well as the greater Grace Chapel staff and family. His patient endurance, detailed work ethic, and writing skills are a dream come true for me. I am indebted to him for his collaboration on this project. Profound thanks to you, Wayne!

The Grace Chapel staff is the best church staff in the world. Love, commitment, passion, and excellence describe them all. I acknowledge your contribution to this book and to my life. God bless you for your dedication!

Thank you to Robert Wolgemuth and staff for their faithful representation at every turn, for every idea, and for catching the vision of this book. Thank you to the Bethany House team for all your humility, professionalism, and cooperation. You made the process wonderful.

Introduction

This world is a mess. It doesn't matter where you look, what you read, or the news channel you prefer, everywhere things seem to get worse and worse. Just a quick review is proof. Unemployment is at high levels, divorce rates continue to climb, families struggle, addiction and natural disasters bombard and paralyze people. We're afraid to go to the mall or even take our kids to school because of what might happen.

Many feel a level of despair. People are looking for answers, and many of them aren't finding any. The truth is Jesus is the answer, and when believers understand His eternal perspective and share it with others, needs are met, hope is given, and everything changes!

Ironically, the apostle Paul faced many of the same issues in the city of Philippi as we do today. Philippi was a big city, and its citizens had all the problems and concerns of anyone in such an environment. There was tremendous pressure from the outside as well as from the inside, not unlike the church today. The church faced the possibility of internal strife (Philippians

1:28–29) and disagreements (4:2–3) and a threat from outside rival teachers who taught a message different from the gospel of Christ (3:18).

There were all kinds of distractions and temptations that tried to pull believers away from the will of God.

For Paul, Philippi was a place with painful memories. In this city he was arrested and beaten. He was placed in stocks and humiliated in front of crowds of people. Even with these harsh circumstances, Paul chose to have an eternal, heavenly perspective and continued to meet people's needs and give them hope. A jailer, and then his whole household, came to Christ as a result of Paul's painful yet steadfast witness for Jesus.

In Philippians 1:11 Paul encourages the church to do the same thing. He wasn't interested in their simply going to church and passively sitting around. He wanted them to know the joy of producing fruit—seeing the Kingdom of God expand in their lives and through their lives. Paul's fruit came as he faithfully shared the gospel. He literally gave his life so others could hear about Jesus. In this intensely personal letter he encourages the people—citizens faced with many of the same issues we are faced with today—to step out into the harvest field, the world around them, and make a difference in someone's life for Jesus' sake.

This next fact might surprise you. As committed as Paul was to reaching people for Jesus, Paul was a man who lived a conflicted life; he was torn between heaven and earth. For him to remain alive meant benefit to many, many people, but beyond that, to be with Jesus in heaven was much better than anything he could possibly experience here on earth (Philippians 1:21–24). Paul's heart was passionately fixed on heaven while his hand was purposefully working to produce fruit. Paul's dilemma is the focus of this book's teaching. Over the next few pages you'll discover, as Paul did, the joy of having your heart rooted and grounded in heaven. You're going to understand its glory and beauty. You'll read about the hope of heaven, your ultimate home. You'll see how heaven heals your hurts. You'll come to appreciate its promises and how a heavenly focus will lead you to a renewed faith, encouragement, and a life that is full.

You'll also learn why this heavenly mind-set matters today. There are wide-open opportunities to reach out to people in this broken world who are ready to hear the good news of Jesus Christ. You see, when your heart is in heaven, you begin

Paul's heart was passionately fixed on heaven while his hand was purposefully working to produce fruit.

to see as Jesus saw. You'll see people who have deep hurts and unmet needs who are desperate for a Savior. You, like Paul, will be torn. You'll desire to be in heaven and be a part of all that God has for you there, but at the same time you'll see people who need your help here.

Heart in heaven, hand in the harvest. That's exactly what God wants from each of us.

I'm excited you are reading this book. It will give you Jesus' perspective in a world gone mad. It will help you set your heart where there is hope, and it will help you give hope to people who so desperately need it.

May God richly bless you.

1

A Renewed Heavenly Vision

Heavenly Focus

Heaven became intensely personal to my wife, Sarah, and me in August of 2009 when a one-person car accident sent our son Josiah to heaven. I'm a pastor, so heaven wasn't a new concept or something I hadn't thought about previously. But, as you would expect, this one moment in time forever changed us. It has served to increase our passion for heaven and has changed our attitudes about how life should be lived while we're on earth.

Josiah—a strong, vibrant young man—was just about to begin his freshman year at the University of Tennessee. Like many young men and women his age, Josiah lived at full throttle. His entire life was ahead of him.

His sudden passing has significantly shaped our lives. Our family clung to one another during those difficult times as never before, and Josiah's memorial service inspired not just a church community but the wider middle Tennessee area as well. Most of all, Josiah's passing lit a fire under me to teach about heaven with a renewed passion.

Our son, unbeknownst to us, signed up as an organ donor. I'll elaborate more on the significance of this later in the book, but for now, simply understand that this one act deeply affected us. Why? Because it was a clear example to me that not only was Josiah serious about Jesus, but he also loved people enough to (literally) give himself away. *His hands were open to people's needs because his heart was in the right place.*

Josiah's passing lit a fire under me to teach about heaven with a renewed passion.

Before going too far with Josiah's story, let me share a few things about myself. I became a Christian at age nineteen, and I've been a pastor for nearly twenty-five years. In those years, heaven has been increasingly important and critical to my faith, teaching, and life. Heaven and our eventual joyous homecoming as Christians are great truths that should be something you and I long for. As a pastor, I get excited when I think about being with God and worshiping Him for eternity. How cool will it be to sit with Paul? Or talk with the apostle John about his time with Jesus and the divine inspiration for the book of Revelation? Or visit with other more contemporary heroes of the faith like Charles H. Spurgeon, C. S. Lewis, or A. W. Tozer? It will be a homecoming and family reunion experience like we can't even imagine.

Heaven is a real place for the believer, and it has at least some place in most everyone's life and thinking. But many think about it whimsically, or only when a life-altering event happens, and throughout everyday life it's tucked away neatly in a mental file folder.

Josiah's passing served as a tremendous shock and reboot in my desire for heaven. As I look back over the last several years I realize that God has gradually opened my eyes and deepened my understanding about heaven. I trace the beginning of these experiences to a moment about fifteen years ago when I received a phone call from my brother Patrick.

I dearly love my older brother and I always welcome his advice and mentoring. I was surprised to hear him weeping on the other end of the phone. He quickly filled me in on what was happening: "Man, I've got a book that I'm reading that is wearing me out. You need to get it." The book he was talking about was *My Dream of Heaven* by Rebecca Ruter Springer. I bought it and read it, and her story floored me. It still floors me today.

Springer's book talks about a spiritual experience she had. Written in 1895 and originally titled *Intra Muros*, it details Springer's very personal, detailed vision of heaven and gives a beautiful glimpse of the eternal home that awaits us. Billy Graham said that the book "captured biblical truths with emotional impressions."[1]

While reading her story, I had one of those moments in my Christian life when the prospect and reality of heaven became markedly clearer. The book challenged me with concepts I'd never known, and provided practical insights that I could share with others who needed help and encouragement.

Fast-forward about seven or eight years, when I began developing a preaching series about heaven. God laid on my heart a desire to help my congregation know and understand the full blessing, joy, and hope that is theirs in heaven. As often happens in my ministry, though I was the one communicating and sharing these messages with the congregation, it seemed God was doing the most powerful work in *my* life. He expanded my knowledge and hunger for heaven. And He also gave me an overwhelming desire to communicate it to all who would listen.

As a part of my research and preparation for that series, I read Randy Alcorn's book simply titled *Heaven*. It's a phenomenal book—probably the most comprehensive book that's been written on the topic. Through it, I learned and understood even more about our eternal home. Randy's book clearly supported a number of thoughts with which I wanted to challenge my congregation. As I studied and learned, I came to realize that Christians often hold numerous misconceptions and unbiblical assumptions about heaven. For example, in heaven we will not merely be up in the sky, floating on a cloud, bored out of our minds and plucking a harp. Heaven is a place; there's exciting supernatural activity, worshiping God, ruling and reigning with Jesus, being reunited with our loved ones, and meeting saints we've only heard of. It's anything but boring.

Christians often hold numerous misconceptions and unbiblical assumptions about heaven.

Randy also points out that rarely do we hear pastors accurately describing heaven as the new earth, which contains trees and rivers, and where resurrected people live in resurrected bodies on a resurrected earth with a resurrected Savior. Many pastors tragically miss this point, and I didn't want to be one of those misinformed pastors with a misguided congregation. No way.

When Josiah went to heaven, everything was taken to a whole new personal level. Since then, not a day has gone by when Sarah and I haven't talked about eternity and the things we've read in the Scriptures about heaven. We can't help but make it a focus of our study, and more important, our lives. When we have the opportunity to speak at an event, we're going to talk about heaven. When we hear about a tragic occurrence, our desire is to help people understand the beauty and fullness of heaven and how we need to live with an eternal perspective so we can find hope and healing in the midst of the tragedy.

Over the next few chapters I hope to give you some new perspectives and help you see heaven in a solidly biblical, yet perhaps unique way. I want to share my passion and help you develop a similar passion. At the same time, I hope to help you find the joy and purpose that comes from living here and now with this new perspective. We're on this journey together, and I can't wait to walk through it with you.

A New Understanding

When Vanderbilt Medical Center was on the other end of the phone, we knew it wasn't good news.

In Nashville and the surrounding area, Vanderbilt is the place where the difficult cases go. I've received a fair share of calls summoning Sarah and me to Vanderbilt, but always to comfort and help people in our congregation and other friends. This time, however, it was our turn to be comforted by others. After receiving that call and racing to the hospital, we spent hours on our faces in prayer for a miracle, but God had other plans. Three days after the accident, on Josiah's nineteenth birthday, we released our son to heaven.

In the immediate whirlwind surrounding Josiah's passing, we cried, we remembered, we prayed, and we grieved. We were surrounded by well-meaning people who did their best to comfort and help us in the midst of our pain.

As we walked through the grief after Josiah passed, all Sarah and I could think to do was pray and look for truth in our

Bibles. What we heard during that time (and what we continue to hear) from God is that the church doesn't know how to deal with "death" biblically. We deal with it culturally, we deal with it traditionally, but we don't deal with it biblically. We learned that lesson from experience. We were just as guilty; there was a gulf in our thinking as well.

Right after Josiah passed we received hundreds of cards, books, and messages from people. The point of many of those messages was that we'd "lost" something. We'd hear, "We're sorry you *lost* Josiah." But what we came to realize is that we didn't lose him! We know exactly where our son went (and still is)! Have we stopped being sad completely? *No.* Do we miss him? *Without question.* We've spent many days and nights in tears of sorrow, but ultimately we haven't lost sight of where Josiah is: alive and in the arms of God.

> *We've spent many days and nights in tears of sorrow, but ultimately we haven't lost sight of where Josiah is: alive and in the arms of God.*

Jesus conquered death (Hebrews 2:14), yet many well-meaning Christians still focus on loss and dying. This breaks my heart, and it's only one example of the misunderstandings about heaven. I'm committed to helping people get it right by relating to those who are in the depths of grief the hope, comfort, and healing God's Word assures.

Paul writes, "If then you were raised with Christ, seek those things which are above, where Christ is, sitting at the right hand of God. Set your mind on things above, not on things on the earth" (Colossians 3:1–2). It's time to become heavenly minded and understand exactly what that means. It's time to talk biblically about heaven because we're missing opportunities to receive and share hope, to extend our hands to help others in need. It is not just those who are grieving that need a heavenly perspective; it's *every believer* (we'll look at this more in later chapters). Unfortunately, many Christians have moved away from the foundational hope that Jesus came to give us—the reality of eternal life with Him in heaven.

Josiah's Story

Josiah couldn't wait to begin his new phase of life at the University of Tennessee, and one day—as his departure approached and with a twinkle in his eye—he said to us, "I don't want to hurt your feelings, but I am so ready to be outta here!"

Sarah and I didn't share his exuberance about the upcoming change at quite the same level, but we were excited for him and prayed expectantly that God would show him direction and wisdom in this time of transition. We wanted to do what we could to encourage and help him, and above all, what was right before the Lord.

We sure didn't know it at the time, but the Lord was preparing us for a different type of separation. His Holy Spirit was preparing us for that call from Vanderbilt and the events that followed.

Even today we don't know many details of the accident, and we don't feel we need to know. What we do know is that it happened on a winding country road in the fog and less than fifteen minutes from our home. It was a one-car accident, and remarkably, his body was in perfect condition—not one stitch, nothing broken . . . except he suffered a serious and fatal brain injury.

For three days, we prayed the Lazarus prayer found in John 11:1–44. In that passage, the story of Lazarus is recounted with the moving pleadings of Mary and Martha to have Jesus resurrect their brother. Miraculously, He did, and that's what we were desperate for as well. We pleaded, "*Please*, Lord, bring our son back to us. Resurrect him, Lord." But that didn't happen.

We firmly believe God answers prayers of faith if they are part of His plan. We knew God could raise our son, and we knew He could heal and restore the whole situation. This was absolutely what we and all our friends and family wanted, but that was not God's plan. Although His answer was not what we wanted, we had to submit ourselves to His sovereign plan, knowing that His plan was better than ours. We had to face the painful reality that our prayers would not be answered the way we wanted. We had to come to grips with God's perfect will and seek His comfort and grace. In His mercy, God has since taught us that Josiah's passing wasn't an end, but simply a continuation of His remarkable plan for our son and for us.

The Donor Revelation

On the morning of the second day of our Vanderbilt vigil, faith was high, prayer was nonstop, and worship was passionate. Many from our church staff and congregation had gathered at the medical center, and Vanderbilt was gracious to give us the space we needed.

Sarah and I awoke that day, literally crawling off the floor of one of Vanderbilt's conference rooms. People whom we loved surrounded us and we deeply felt their compassion, prayers, and support, and we did not relent from asking God for a miracle.

However, we also thought it would be prudent to talk with the Donor Services office because we had so many pressing questions about what to do should God take Josiah to heaven. So, just forty-eight hours after the accident, we began moving toward a decision of donating Josiah's organs, because we knew that's what he'd want us to do. In his almost nineteen years of life, it was clear that Josiah held a deep desire and concern for others. His compassion and love were a challenge in my own life.

So that night, the wonderful people from Vanderbilt's Donor Services met with us. In our minds—and we'd been bracing ourselves for this—there was a chance that we would soon be giving them permission to harvest Josiah's unharmed organs. Trust me, it's not an experience or decision you ever want to have to make. After sitting down, the head of Donor Services opened the file folder he had with him and pulled out a piece of paper. He handed Sarah the document and said, "As you can see, your son is a donor." We were stunned. I thought we were sitting down to make the hardest decision of our lives, but the decision had already been made. Going into that meeting we were convinced that Josiah would want to be a donor, but it was going to be very difficult to follow through on that conviction, especially just two days removed from the accident.

When the man from Donor Services held up that paper and let us know that Josiah had made that decision after his eighteenth birthday, Sarah and I looked at each other and knew that Josiah's wishes would be honored. Our burden of making that decision had been lifted.

Josiah's decision not only relieved a tremendous burden from us, it clearly showed us that our son's heart was in heaven long before he arrived there that fateful night. As I wrote earlier, Josiah loved Jesus and he loved people. His selfless decision clearly reflected his heart and his attitude.

On the afternoon of August 14, 2009, the exact day of Josiah's nineteenth birthday and three days after he entered Vanderbilt hospital, we talked with the chief neurosurgeon. He confirmed Josiah's condition and informed us that there were people waiting, as we spoke, for his organs to save their lives.

Reflecting on the emotion of that decision—a mere seventy-two hours after our perfectly healthy, strong, life-in-front-of-him son bounded out the door to meet some friends—still overwhelms me.

On his nineteenth birthday, we honored Josiah's decision.

Hard-Pressed Living

As I've spent time thinking back over the meeting with Donor Services and the resulting organ donation, Josiah's actions challenge me with an example of how we should live our lives as believers. Because his heart was in heaven, he lived every day with an eternal perspective. As Dee Brestin wrote, a heart in heaven means that we "understand the importance of valuing the eternal over the transitory."[2] It means putting our focus on the things of God that have eternal value rather than the things of this earth that can easily rust, perish, or be destroyed instantly in a tornado or other disaster.

Our son's heart was in heaven long before he arrived there that fateful night.

But as Josiah showed me, when our hearts are focused on heaven and we live with this eternal perspective, it's only natural that our hands are in the harvest—helping people who are desperate for a personal encounter with the love of God.

In John 4:35 Jesus says, "Do you not say, 'There are still four months and then comes the harvest'? Behold, I say to you, lift up your eyes and look at the fields, for they are already white for harvest!"

Unlike those of us living in the twenty-first century, Jesus' disciples knew exactly what He was saying. They knew the significance of the harvest season—it was a time to roll up your sleeves and work. There was finally an opportunity to bring in the crops whose seeds had been sown and cultivated months ago. It was a time of hard labor and celebration. It was a time of reward. When Jesus called for eyes to be lifted up, He wanted His followers to see those around them; Jesus wanted them "harvested" into His Kingdom. He wanted them helped, served, and made aware of His saving grace.

It might seem as though a heart focused on heaven and hands focused on the harvest can't coexist. It might seem like an either/or option, but we're called to live in this holy tension. Paul wrote in Philippians 1:23–24, "I am hard-pressed between the two [heaven and earth], having a desire to depart and be with Christ, *which is far better*. Nevertheless to remain in the flesh is more needful for you" (emphasis mine). These powerful verses form the essence and inspirational key for this book.

When our hearts are focused on heaven and we live with this eternal perspective, it's only natural that our hands are in the harvest.

Yes, I want desperately to be with Jesus in heaven, *and yes*, I see and want to meet the needs of others here and now.

Paul's life is a great example of this hard-pressed living between heaven and earth. He was eager to be with Jesus, convinced that being in the physical presence of Christ was far better than life on earth. But it was actually this heavenly perspective that drove him to minister, serve, and be excited about staying.

We think it would do the opposite. In our natural, earthly influenced mind, we think, *Paul was so heavenly minded that he must have been no earthly good.* But that's not the case. In

29

fact, it was just the opposite. He was so heavenly minded that it propelled him to be of tremendous earthly good. Over two thousand years later, people are still learning and experiencing massive life changes because of Paul's letters and example. His heavenly, hard-pressed mind-set left a legacy of earthly good.

William Barclay wrote about the word *depart* used in the letter to the Philippians:

> The word [Paul] uses is *senechomai*, the word which would be used of a traveler in a narrow passage, with a wall of rock on either side, unable to turn off in any direction and able only to go straight on. For himself, he wanted to depart and to be with Christ; for the sake of his friends, and of what he could do with them and for them, he wanted to be left in this life. . . . Paul's desire to live is not for his own sake, but for the sake of those whom he can continue to help.[3]

That's hard-pressed living!

Life Change

After Josiah passed, we found a letter he wrote to himself during a summer break three years earlier. It describes a breakthrough he had with the Lord during a time of prayer. In the letter, he wrote that he wanted to influence people for God when he returned to high school in the fall. He wanted to love people and show them his deep appreciation for them. God heard Josiah's cry and answered his prayer. In fact, God is still answering that prayer. God was and is faithful to that cry of Josiah's heart.

Josiah's decision to become an organ donor immediately rescued five lives. And we've learned that a total of seventy-seven people ultimately benefited from his decision. We know that the man who received his heart was fifty-five at the time, with five grandchildren. Today, he's alive and in good health. We know the people who received his kidneys and have been told, "Josiah saved their lives." Through them, Josiah's work on earth (his hand in the harvest) continues.

A tremendous amount of spiritual work happened in the span of three days in the halls of Vanderbilt Medical Center as God radically touched many of Josiah's friends. We witnessed them trusting God and crying out to Him, all while loving and serving our family and one another. And that work hasn't stopped.

As I write this, we have finished building two of four homes housing orphaned boys in the Dominican Republic. Collectively they are called "Josiah's House." In his time on earth, we often marveled at Josiah's heart for children, particularly orphans and underprivileged kids, and we began this project in his honor after he passed. We know that this project is bringing him tremendous joy as he looks down from heaven.

Josiah's decision to become an organ donor immediately rescued five lives.

So don't be afraid or apprehensive about how a heavenly perspective will change you. From my experience, it will only serve to grow your faith and help you rely totally and absolutely on God.

☙⚬

Sarah and I could not have navigated the tough waters without the faith and trust in God that's rooted in a heavenly perspective. There isn't a day that passes where we don't think about our son, and—make no mistake—some days are incredibly trying. Yet ultimately, we rest in our God's comfort, peace, and love.

We did not receive the miracle we asked for, but God is faithful. And because Josiah lived with a heavenly perspective, his generous spirit brought life and hope to people he'd never even met.

This is a life-changing book. I know that because having my eyes opened to hard-pressed living has changed *my* life and the lives of those around me. It will challenge you to live life with a perspective and mission radically different from what the world offers. It will encourage you and help you discover how you can live your life to its fullest and richest.

In the next few chapters we'll dive more deeply into what a heavenly perspective means, and we'll let Scripture guide our journey. We'll see the glory of heaven beautifully revealed and we'll discover the biblical call for hands in the harvest. And once you develop that perspective, you'll naturally be hard-pressed between the two, and discover a new and marvelous way to live your Christian life.

2

A Passion for Hard-Pressed Living

An Intense Longing

I love Psalm 84:1–2, 10. David wrote:

> How lovely is Your tabernacle, O Lord of hosts! My soul longs, yes, even faints for the courts of the Lord; My heart and my flesh cry out for the living God. . . . For a day in Your courts is better than a thousand. I would rather be a doorkeeper in the house of my God than dwell in the tents of wickedness.

His soul is yearning deeply for God's presence. His heart is ready to break with desire to worship God and spend time in His presence. David was torn between two lives—one in heaven in the presence of God and the other his life here on this earth.

He shows us this tearing again in Psalm 23. He writes how he longs to have God lead him "beside the still waters" here on earth and "dwell in the house of the Lord forever" in heaven. The warrior king desperately wanted the comfort and rest of home, yet he also wanted the comfort, peace, and rest of God. He was torn between the two. He was desperate for both.

When we dig into Paul's life, we see a picture of that same longing. His life fills the canvas with the *what* and the *why* of hard-pressed living (having our hearts in heaven and our hands in the harvest) and also clearly depicts why it was so important to him.

The key Bible verses for this fresh perspective are found in the first chapter of Philippians. However, before we go there, we need to see why Paul's heart longed to be in heaven and why he longed to have his hand in the harvest.

A Radical Conversion

Getting a clear picture of hard-pressed living starts with the apostle Paul's conversion. In approximately 35 AD, something radical happened to Paul (at that time named Saul of Tarsus).

The Bible gives us a rude introduction to Paul. We first meet him at the stoning of Stephen in Acts 7 and 8. He's one of the Jewish leaders who takes part in the brutal and bloody murder of this brave Christian leader, and Scripture describes Paul (Saul) as "consenting to his death" (Acts 8:1).

By Acts chapter 9 Saul is on the prowl to persecute more Christians. Pastor Charles Swindoll wrote:

Saul's blood is boiling. He's on a murderous rampage toward Damascus. He charged north out of Jerusalem with the fury of Alexander the Great sweeping across Persia, and the determined resolve of William Tecumseh Sherman in his scorching march across Georgia. Saul was borderline out of control. His fury had intensified almost to the point of no return. Such bloodthirsty determination and blind hatred for the followers of Christ, drove him hard toward his distant destination: Damascus.[1]

But something happened on the way to Damascus.

Have you ever been on a journey, driving down the freeway toward your destination, when something happens that completely changes your plans? You are heading one way and suddenly, out of nowhere, you find yourself making different turns and going a new direction? I know it's happened to me; my story in chapter 1 was one of those times.

Something like that happened to Paul.

When we read Acts 9:1–8, we see that Paul's plans changed radically. He saw a heavenly light, he heard a heavenly voice, and he was immediately sent on a heavenly mission. This was the beginning of Paul's new hard-pressed lifestyle, having his heart in heaven and his hand in the harvest.

Why was his heart so quickly focused on heaven? The answer is in one word: Jesus. Paul so easily and eagerly committed his heart to having a heavenly focus because of the mercy, forgiveness, redemption, and kindness that Jesus, the Son of God, showed to a murderer. Paul's heart instantly went to heaven because of this incredible loving-kindness of Jesus Christ *from* heaven. This is also why, after hearing from the Lord, he said, "Lord, what do you want me to do?"

> *Paul's heart instantly went to heaven because of this incredible loving-kindness of Jesus Christ from heaven.*

Heaven changed Paul's heart; therefore, his hand was ready to work in the harvest.

Paul immediately began to preach Jesus Christ as the Savior, Messiah, and Son of God in the synagogues (Acts 9:20). Can you imagine the wonder this brought to the Jews in Damascus? The man who was once a principal leader against Jesus and His followers was now preaching that He is the Son of God in their synagogues. Here's the deal: Once heaven really touches your heart, your hand will *really* be in the harvest.

A Radical Intensity

We fast-forward twenty-one years. Paul writes in 1 Corinthians 2:9–10:

> As it is written: "Eye has not seen, nor ear heard, nor have entered into the heart of man the things which God has prepared for those who love Him." But God has revealed them to us through His Spirit. For the Spirit searches all things, yes, the deep things of God.

All those years after he saw the heavenly light, heard the heavenly voice, and went on a heavenly mission, Paul is still learning and growing. Heaven is not getting any further away from him. He's not pushing it into the background of his mind. His heart is still deeply rooted in heaven and the things of heaven, and after twenty-one years he wants more. Paul's heart for eternity only intensified.

I pray that this would always be true of us. I pray that heaven would not simply become a great concept that was very real when we said yes to Jesus, then sometime later—ten weeks or ten years—went by the wayside. I pray that like Paul we would say, "God, give me more. Help me see heaven as more meaningful, more powerful, more intimate, and lovelier than ever before." Our heart in heaven needs to grow and mature, and we should never stop asking God to reveal the deep things to us.

A Radical Presence

In the same year (approximately 56 AD), Paul wrote his second letter to the Corinthians. He wrote in 2 Corinthians 12:1–4:

It is doubtless not profitable for me to boast. I will come to visions and revelations of the Lord: I know a man in Christ who fourteen years ago—whether in the body I do not know, or whether out of the body I do not know, God knows—such a one was caught up to the third heaven. And I know such a man—whether in the body or out of the body I do not know, God knows—how he was caught up into Paradise and heard inexpressible words, which it is not lawful for a man to utter.

While Paul is being humble, he's actually writing about his own personal experience. Amazingly, he had been caught up in the third heaven, where God dwells (the first heaven being the air we breathe and where birds fly, the second being the sun, moon, and stars). Paul was caught up in the paradise of God.

Paul's timing is fascinating. He says he was caught up into the third heaven fourteen years earlier. He wrote 1 Corinthians just months earlier—why didn't he tell us about this at that point? Scripture unfortunately doesn't tell us. However, I do know this: being caught up into the third heaven is what allowed Paul to write, "'Eye has not seen, nor ear heard, nor have entered into the heart of man the things which God has prepared for those who love Him.' But God has revealed them to us through His Spirit."

This is a picture of the hard-pressed lifestyle. Paul's heart was in heaven and his hand was in the harvest because of what had been revealed to him *from* heaven at his conversion and what had been revealed *about* heaven when he was caught up there. He saw God's presence in radical ways.

It should be no different for us. This hard-pressed lifestyle should be our standard if we follow Jesus. You may not have had a heavenly light shine on you, but you've seen the light. You may not have heard a heavenly voice, but you've read God's Word. You may not have been sent on a heavenly mission to

Damascus, but you've been sent out in the Great Commission (Matthew 28) and your hand should be in the harvest. Living the hard-pressed life is nonnegotiable!

A Radical Lifestyle

Four years later Paul writes to the church of Colosse,

> If then you were raised with Christ, seek those things which are above, where Christ is, sitting at the right hand of God. Set your mind on things above, not on things on the earth. For you died, and your life is hidden with Christ in God. When Christ who is our life appears, then you also will appear with Him in glory.
>
> Colossians 3:1–4

He's writing twenty-five years after his conversion. Decades after the heavenly light, the heavenly voice, and the heavenly mission, he says to the people of Colosse, "Seek those things which are above." He implores them to pursue the things of heaven—to hunt them and go after them with everything they have.

Beloved, you are going to live in heaven forever. Isn't it time you knew something about it? Paul says, "While you're on this earth, let heaven be a focal point and filter for your thoughts, let heaven give you eternal perspective for your earthly life."

Paul asks us to seek and set our minds above—not on—the things of this earth. He knows that, unfortunately, we know a lot more about this earth than we do heaven. He knows that, too often, this earth is our thing, it's our ring, and it's our bling. We're focused on what we have and what we'd like to have here on earth.

We don't know enough about heaven because we're not open to what the Spirit is trying to teach us. In 1 Corinthians 2:9 Paul writes, "Eye hasn't seen, nor ear heard, nor has it even entered into the heart of man the things that God has prepared for those that love Him" (my paraphrase). Typically, we stop reading right there and form an opinion that heaven is unknowable. However, the next verse says, "The Spirit has revealed to us the deep things of God" (my paraphrase). Clearly, we have to let the Holy Spirit teach us about

This hard-pressed lifestyle should be our standard if we follow Jesus.

what God has prepared for us in heaven. Beloved, that's only going to happen when we get our minds off the things of this earth and set them on the things above, where Christ is, at the right hand of God.

What have you set your mind on? What have you given your heart to? What's important to you?

When you have a biblical understanding of heaven, things change. Paul knew that and so must we.

Twenty-five years after the apostle Paul had his dramatic conversion experience, he was still living a radical lifestyle and hammering his point to the people. He was still preaching *about* and living *with* heaven in his heart and his hand in the harvest.

Radical Questions

We've seen a picture of hard-pressed living in Paul. He sought after heaven and a heavenly perspective, and he did all he could to help other people do the same.

I'm going to ask a few questions that you need to answer honestly:

- If you know Jesus Christ as your personal Savior, is heaven your treasure, or is it simply a part-time afterthought, something you only think about occasionally?

- If you don't know Jesus Christ, have you thought about eternity? Are you ready to entrust your life to Jesus Christ forever? If you are ready, please see pages 80–82 for how you can do this today.
- Is heaven what you are seeking and have your mind set on? Do you have an eternal perspective? Do you see your life here on earth through the lens of eternity?
- Is your hand in the harvest because your heart is in heaven?

Here's a fact: When people really meet Jesus, their hearts so love, adore, and respond to what He has done for them from heaven that it affects how they live here on earth. It affects whom they serve and how they serve. They don't live a self-centered, self-empowered life. They can't *not* talk about Him and they can't *not* serve Him. Has Jesus, the Son of God, converted your life, and is your conversion evidenced by changed outward behavior toward others?

I would lovingly, humbly, and biblically tell you that if you say that your heart is in heaven and for Jesus, and there is no outward loving and serving of others and reaching people for the Kingdom, your heart truly isn't there. You have a form of godliness, but you've resisted the power of Jesus fully touching your own life (2 Timothy 3:5).

I can't find examples of people who have radical encounters with Jesus and then don't reach out to other people.

I can't find examples of people who have radical encounters with Jesus and then don't reach out to other people. I can't find people who have their hearts in heaven and, at the same time, don't have their hands in the harvest.

It's not okay for us to have calloused buns from sitting on pews and not calloused hands from helping people. It is not okay for us to be spiritually unproductive.

40

Examine yourself. Do a checkup. If you profess Jesus and your hand isn't in the harvest, find a way to get involved. Find a way to communicate the life change you've experienced by loving and serving others. Then you will display a more complete picture of the hard-pressed life.

Paul's Purpose

The apostle Paul had a passion for life. He was a completely different man after his remarkable Damascus Road conversion, and he passionately and diligently sought after Jesus. Commentator F. F. Bruce, quoting British New Testament scholar James D. G. Dunn, wrote,

> What happened on the Damascus road was no isolated mystical experience, no mere "flash of insight or intellectual conviction, but a personal encounter, the beginning of a personal relationship which became the dominating passion of his life. . . . Religious experience for Paul is basically experience of union with Christ."[2]

Paul was torn between two desires—wanting to be with Jesus while at the same time wanting to share Jesus with others. This passion drove him to talk about Jesus, serve others in the name of Jesus, and ultimately give his life for Jesus.

Living for Christ

Paul wrote in Philippians 1:21–25:

> To me, to live is Christ, and to die is gain. But if I live on in the flesh, this will mean fruit from my labor; yet what I shall choose I cannot tell. For I am hard-pressed between the two, having a

desire to depart and be with Christ, which is far better. Nevertheless to remain in the flesh is more needful for you. And being confident of this, I know that I shall remain and continue with you all for your progress and joy of faith.

When we unpack this passage we discover the essence of Paul's passion. For Paul, living was for Christ. For him, and for us, it means doing God's will regardless of the personal cost or blessing. Paul's purpose, cause, and stand—literally everything about him—was to live for Christ.

Living for Christ has nothing to do with our occupation. We think our lives are defined by a job or career, but our true identities are found in Christ and living for Christ. Authentic Christian living is not about what we do; it's about who we are and whom we serve.

Paul wrote something similar to the church in Galatia: "I have been crucified with Christ; it is no longer I who live, but Christ lives in me; and the life which I now live in the flesh I live by faith in the Son of God, who loved me and gave Himself for me" (Galatians 2:20).

Witness Lee tells a story that illustrates what it means to live for Christ:

During the Boxer Rebellion in China, hundreds of Christians were martyred. One day in Peking, the old capital of China, the Boxers were parading down the street. Sitting in the back of a wagon was a young Christian woman who was being led away to be executed. She was surrounded by executioners with swords in their hands. The atmosphere was terrifying, filled with the shoutings of the Boxers. Nevertheless, her face was glowing as she was singing praises to the Lord. This young woman could be filled with praises in the midst of such a terrifying situation because faith was working within her. She was filled with appreciation of the Lord Jesus. Because she loved Him so much, He spontaneously became the faith within her. This faith produced an organic union in which she was joined to the Lord.[3]

Like Paul, she chose to give her life to Christ because He loved her and gave His life for her. This woman put her hand in the harvest (one man came to Christ and became a preacher of the gospel in China because of her witness) because Jesus loved her and she wanted to live for Him.

We can do the same. Because Jesus loves us and gave Himself up for us, we can return the gift and give our lives for Him.

Dying Is Gain

When we live for Christ, "to die is gain" (Philippians 1:21). If we don't live for Christ, dying is hell.

For the Christian, dying isn't loss; dying is gain. It is then that we enter into the prepared promise, presence, and paradise of God. Christians essentially graduate from life to Life.

This may be new thinking for you. Unfortunately, many Christians have been conditioned by our culture and tradition to think that life is here on this earth. We need to take a closer look into Scripture and realize that simply isn't true. Paul says to live is Christ and to die is gain. Why? Because when we trust Jesus as our Savior, we're going to enter that very place for which we were originally created. Our spirits were not meant to live in this world. They were meant to live in a resurrected Eden-like body in a place we can't come close to imagining—in the presence and paradise of the living God.

> *Because Jesus loves us and gave Himself up for us, we can return the gift and give our lives for Him.*

As beautiful as this earth is, with its purple mountains majesty, fruited plains, and shining seas, we were not saved to live here. We were not created for this place. We are just passing through this world on our way to God's heaven. I can't wait.

Therefore, living our Christian lives looking forward to the reward of the promise, presence, and paradise of God is vital. Far too many Christians are transitioning into heaven and looking back over their lives saying, "I wish I would have served God more, loved God more, and brought more people with me to heaven." They look back over their lives with regret, and the fact is, we don't have to do that. We can intentionally and purposefully live a hard-pressed life; then we don't look back with regret but look forward to the reward.

How? By realizing, as Paul did, that how we live on this earth determines our future reward.

Being saved isn't just having the hope of heaven; that's the very beginning point. It's how we live after we're saved—how productive and fruitful we are in loving and serving others—that matters and determines our reward from Jesus. How we live every day, whether we realize it or not, sows seeds into eternity. We're either sowing worthwhile seeds that produce fruit, or we're sowing worthless seeds that have no eternal value.

In Matthew 6:19–20 Jesus says,

> Do not lay up for yourselves treasures on earth, where moth and rust destroy and where thieves break in and steal; but lay up for yourselves treasures in heaven, where neither moth nor rust destroys and where thieves do not break in and steal.

He's telling us not to be earthly minded. He's telling us not to have our hearts focused on this earth (including its values and traditions). He wants our hearts focused on heavenly treasure.

44

When we do, we won't live in regret. We will be living for Jesus and knowing that dying is our gain. We'll have a heart focused on heaven and live with a heavenly perspective on everything. We'll know our rewards are secure because we've reached out to others in the love, compassion, and power of Jesus.

Paul's Motivation

Author and Pastor Henry Blackaby wrote, "Paul the Apostle said, 'The love of Christ compels [me]' (2 Corinthians 5:14). He knew God had an eternal purpose for his life."[4]

The apostle Paul was motivated by a deep understanding that he would be judged for future rewards based upon how he lived his life while on this earth.

He writes in 2 Corinthians 5:8–10,

> We are confident, yes, well pleased rather to be absent from the body and to be present with the Lord. Therefore we make it our aim, whether present or absent, to be well pleasing to Him. For we must all appear before the judgment seat of Christ, that each one may receive the things done in the body, according to what he has done, whether good or bad.

We need to pay particular attention to the last word of this verse. *Bad* doesn't mean "awful" or "terrible"; it means "worthless." It has a connotation of something that has no value. As Christians, we are all going to appear before the judgment seat of Christ, not for salvation but for reward. Paul made it his aim to please God and accomplish things that bring value to others—things that reflect the heart of God and are worthwhile.

How we live every day, whether we realize it or not, sows seeds into eternity.

45

We need to think about standing before Jesus and giving an account of our lives. As we do, we should seriously reflect on our life here on earth and whether what we are doing has worth from an eternal perspective. It's important that we, like Paul, refuse to give our lives to things that are eternally worthless and selfish. Paul understood this completely and it motivated him, and it needs to motivate us.

The thought of the judgment seat (or *bema* seat,[5] as it's called in Greek) has motivated and shaped the lives of the heroes of the faith for years.

Martin Luther, the Father of Protestantism, felt that the truth of the *bema* seat was so important that for years the only two dates on his calendar were "today" and "that day." Luther knew that if he lived right today, "that day" would take care of itself![6]

General William Booth (founder of the Salvation Army) had a vision of going to heaven and being questioned by people and by Christ about his life on earth. He was so horrified by his answers that he wanted one more chance to return to earth and make amends for a wasted Christian life.[7]

Knowing there are rewards and a final accounting at the *bema* seat for how we live on earth should shape and mold us as well.

As a little girl, Amy Carmichael sensed God whispering 1 Corinthians 3 into her ear. She understood that all of her works would be thrown into the fire, and only those things done for Christ would matter eternally and bring reward. Amy went on to become a missionary to India, opening an orphanage and founding a mission in Dohnavur.[8]

First Corinthians 3 captured her heart, and it should capture ours as well. Paul wrote:

According to the grace of God which was given to me, as a wise master builder I have laid the foundation, and another builds on it. But let each one take heed how he builds on it. For no other foundation can anyone lay than that which is laid, which is Jesus Christ. Now if anyone builds on this foundation with gold, silver, precious stones, wood, hay, straw, each one's work will become clear; for the Day will declare it, because it will be revealed by fire; and the fire will test each one's work, of what sort it is. If anyone's work which he has built on it endures, he will receive a reward. If anyone's work is burned, he will suffer loss; but he himself will be saved, yet so as through fire.

vv. 10–15

Paul is telling us that as wise master builders, we need to build according to a plan. He's carefully calculating a foundation that keeps his heart in heaven and his hand in the harvest.

Starting in verse 12, he shows us different types of building materials. Three survive the judgment fire and three don't survive. He is encouraging us to build our lives on lasting materials—gold, silver, and precious stones. Why not wood, hay, and straw? Because they perish. Using those inferior materials means we're building upon the foundation of Jesus using worthless things. It means we are unwilling to pay the price.

Then, he tells us in verse 13 that every person's work, with the materials with which they've built their spiritual lives, is going to become clear. Jesus Christ, the ultimate and final judge, will declare the worth of our work. Fire will reveal how we've built our spiritual houses.

Improper actions, impure motives, or even right actions with wrong motives are not going to stand the test of God's purifying fire. At some point our spiritual houses will have matches thrown on them. What is worthless will be burned and what is precious will stand and be rewarded.

It saddens me when I realize how many Christians are going to run out of a burning, crumbling spiritual house. No reward, just fire and smoke. Yes, they are saved, but there's no reward. Their motivation was self-centered instead of others-focused. Their hearts weren't focused on heaven; instead, their hearts were focused on the temporary things of this earth, and those things motivated their actions.

On the other hand, some Christians will get rewards and responsibilities in heaven that will blow their minds. Why? Because their hearts were motivated by heaven.

Should this change how we view our lives? Absolutely. We need to be motivated by heaven so that our hands will automatically go out in love and service to others—into the great harvest of people who need Jesus.

Let's not choose the easy way. Let's not go to heaven by the skin of our teeth. Every day we have the ability to build with precious, eternal materials. Let's learn from Paul's motivation and make sure we're constructing with the valuable and not the worthless.

Paul's Attitude

There is a difference between motivation and attitude. Our attitudes shape who we are. Attitude is that mental perspective or emotional stand we've taken about something. Motivation is the ability and energy required to sustain an attitude. Simply said, attitude is the fire and motivation fans the fire.

It's clear from his writing that Paul had a "dying is gain" attitude. It wasn't some hopeless death wish. Quite the contrary, it was an earnest longing to be with Jesus and to receive his reward.

In 2 Corinthians 5:1–5 Paul clearly lays it out for us. He tells us that he earnestly desires his heavenly body and to be in his heavenly home. His desire is for the groanings, burdens, and limitations of this world to be swallowed up by the immortal life of God. He wants to be not just "clothed," but "further clothed." He wants to receive his heavenly body and his heavenly home, to be in that special dwelling place that God originally intended for all of us.

To Paul, heaven was his incredibly awesome eternal home. Paul knew, and we can know as well, that when we get swallowed by life itself, the promise, presence, and paradise of God will converge in our spirit. It's at that moment that we will receive the body that God always intended for us to have. It is then that we will live in the true resurrection life and power of Jesus, in an Eden-like atmosphere. Think about it, walking with God in unhindered communion and relationship. There will be no sorrow, pain, or tears. It is then that we will be fully healed and restored (Revelation 21:3–7; 1 Corinthians 15:35–58; 2 Corinthians 5:1–9; Philippians 3:20–21).

It's clear from his writing that Paul had a "dying is gain" attitude. It wasn't some hopeless death wish.

Dying is indeed gain for the child of God.

This promise is what shaped Paul's attitude, and it needs to shape ours as well. Our personal fire needs to be the incredible longing for heaven and all that is waiting for us. Our attitude should not be rooted in things that originate from this temporary life on earth. If it is, we're caught in Satan's trap and we're standing on worthless promises. We're building our spiritual houses with wood and straw instead of the precious stones of God's promises.

Our attitude needs to be rooted in eternal realities, in the hope of heaven. When it is, we have an incredible longing for heaven. It's a Spirit-led "knowing" that every wrong will be made right; every hurt and wound will be healed. It's an earnest desire that supports us when the pain and sorrow of this earth come knocking, because we know in our hearts that in heaven all the pain and heartache will be gone—forever.

Having our heart in heaven means our attitude is fixed on the fact that, for the Christ-follower, dying is gain.

Paul's Life and Fruit

One of the benefits of living with such a heavenly attitude was that Paul's life produced valuable fruit.

Philippians 1:22 says, "If I live on in the flesh, this will mean fruit from my labor; yet what I shall choose I cannot tell." Clearly, as long as Paul lived on earth, he was going to produce fruit. Paul was determined to expand the Kingdom while he was on earth. His motivation and attitude drove him to put his hands in the harvest. He knew good things would happen because his heart was in the right place.

In Philippians 1:20 he wrote, "According to my earnest expectation and hope that in nothing I shall be ashamed, but with all boldness, as always, so now also Christ will be magnified in my body, whether by life or by death." There was no false humility in Paul. There was nothing out of line with his confidence. He was motivated by heavenly rewards, and he was absolutely positive that he would magnify Jesus to everyone he encountered, wherever he encountered them. Paul was certain Jesus would work in him and through him, making a difference in people's lives, because his heart was set on heaven.

Keep in mind that Paul was in chains when he wrote this letter to the Philippian church—chained to a guard in horrible prison conditions. It was very likely that he would be found guilty of being a traitor to Rome and executed, and he was awaiting the final verdict while writing this letter. But Paul's earnest and single desire was to magnify Christ and bear fruit for His Kingdom. He was not afraid of life or death. Henry and Norman Blackaby wrote,

> When God chose us, He also designed our lives to bear good fruit. This fruit includes our character as well as our service to God in His work. With the strong emphasis Jesus placed on bearing fruit (Luke 13:6–9), it is important to look and see what your life is yielding.[9]

Once our motivation and our attitude are set on heaven, we can, like Paul, be uncomfortable about sticking around on earth, but it's clear that while we're here our lives need to produce lasting, worthwhile fruit. There may be a battle raging in us (heaven or harvest), and it's a hard choice, but we must be rooted in eternity and still extend our hands to others.

Paul's Preoccupation

Paul wrote, "I am hard-pressed between the two, having a desire to depart and be with Christ, which is far better" (Philippians 1:23). The Greek words translated "hard-pressed" literally mean "to be completely preoccupied." Paul was completely preoccupied with this issue of having his heart in heaven (longing to be there) and yet having his hand in the harvest (wanting to produce fruit and serve others). He was continually preoccupied with this thinking and tension.

John MacArthur wrote,

> Preoccupation with the eternal realities that are ours in Christ is to be the pattern of the believer's life. To be preoccupied with

51

heaven is to be preoccupied with the One who reigns there and His purposes, plans, provisions, and power. It is also to view the things, people, and events of this world through His eyes and with an eternal perspective.[10]

A. W. Tozer wrote, "We are called to an everlasting preoccupation with God."[11]

Living the hard-pressed life isn't having an occasional thought about heaven; it's having a *preoccupation* with all it holds for God's beloved.

It's critical for our understanding that we go a bit deeper into what Paul is saying. First, he says, "Let me be clear: I have a *desire*." The beauty of the Greek language allows us to see what this desire really means. It doesn't just mean, "Yeah, that would be cool! I'm kind of hard-pressed; I'm a little intrigued by this heaven thing." No! The term Paul uses for *desire* indicates a longing, an insatiable lust.[12] This word was frequently used to convey that it is almost illegal to want something this badly. To paraphrase Paul: "I have such a longing, a lust-filled desire to go to heaven that it should almost be illegal."

> *While we're here our lives need to produce lasting, worthwhile fruit.*

Second, Paul says, "I have a desire to *depart*." He's not talking about just leaving. The term means "to break camp, to loose ties, to fold my tent or pull the anchor."[13] Paul is pulling up the anchor and setting sail for the glorious promise, presence, and paradise of God. He's breaking camp and pitching his tent in God's eternal home.

Third, he says, "When I depart, I'm going to *be with Christ* because the ultimate reward of heaven is to be with Him." Paul is preoccupied with thoughts of being face-to-face with Jesus. He says it again in 2 Corinthians 5:8: "We are confident, yes, well pleased rather to be absent from the body and to be present with the Lord." He didn't just want to hear His voice; Paul wanted to gaze upon the face that saved him and be in the presence of the One who loved him, called him, and continually blessed him. He was preoccupied with this thought!

Last, he said it was "*far better.*" It was, as the original Greek conveys, "many, much, much better, more useful and more profitable."[14]

That's the kind of difference Paul is talking about. Being with Christ is far, far better than anything on earth.

Ted Dekker wrote,

> Having been given a glimpse of the bliss that awaits us (2 Corinthians 12:4), Paul lived a life obsessed with that day when he would have his full inheritance. Any such encounter with that bliss will surely bend any man to a fanaticism for it. So it is no wonder Paul was so fanatical about the hope of glory.[15]

Paul understood the glory of heaven. His motivation and attitude were rooted there, and he lived with a preoccupation with heaven while he was on this earth.

Paul's Focus

Paul writes in Philippians 1:24–25, "Nevertheless to remain in the flesh is more needful for you. And being confident of this, I know that I shall remain and continue with you all for your progress and joy of faith."

There's a tug-of-war going on inside the apostle Paul. He would rather be in heaven—it's his motivation, the foundation for his attitude, and an obsession for him. However, he ends this part of his epistle by saying, "I think it's better that I remain here, in this body, for you."

Paul wants to move on more than anything; however, his hand is in the harvest. He knows there will be fruit from his labor and that it will be extremely beneficial for other people if he stays right here. He's saying, "I'm going to stay here because you need me. God is making a difference through my life and I want to continue to work for the progress of your joy and faith."

Three families—the Clonts, Krikacs, and Helmsworths—joined us when we moved from Southern California to Leipers Fork, Tennessee. They left family members, friends, and careers to join Sarah and me on this journey. We didn't know anyone in Leipers Fork, but God led us in a new direction and these three families committed themselves to the mission and us. While we know God is building Grace Chapel, we also know that the faithfulness of these friends to remain with us, counsel us, and continue with us in ministry made all the difference. My life, Sarah's life, and the lives of thousands of people have been changed because of the focus and sacrifice of these original three families. Grace Chapel will forever be indebted to these amazing Christians. For Sarah and me, they exemplify Paul's focus: heart in heaven, hand in the harvest.

I want you to think about this: Will you get heavenly minded so you can be of some earthly good? Will you allow your heart to be so captured by the splendor, beauty, and awesomeness of the God of heaven that your life really changes? Will you allow that motivation, attitude, and focus to grip your heart so that you make a decision to serve other people, on this earth, for the Kingdom?

Let's get our hearts in heaven and put out our hands into the harvest. Let's stop making excuses and journey together into this tremendous opportunity that lies before us.

3

Heaven Is Our Real Home

Eternity in Our Hearts

Ecclesiastes 3:11 says that God "has put eternity in [our] hearts." Everything we long for and appreciate that is godly, loving, true, right, peaceful, secure, beautiful, and eternal all goes back to the Garden of Eden and God's intention for humankind—to live forever in a state of beautiful heavenly joy.

Every person, whether they're a Christian or not, has the spiritual DNA of Adam and Eve. It doesn't matter how foul or sinful a person is. It doesn't matter how much they want to deny it and rebel against it; even if they try to suppress the feeling, it's still deeply imbedded within them. There is an understanding, a knowing, that there must be more than life on earth. Pastor and author Max Lucado wrote,

> You were intended to live in your Father's house. Any place less than his is insufficient. Any place far from his is dangerous. Only

the home built for your heart can protect your heart. And your Father wants you to dwell *in* Him.[1]

God wants all of us to be home with Him, and He put this deep longing for His eternity in our hearts. People may not be able to articulate it, but it's there. Many people, without even knowing where the desire comes from, long for it, write about it, sing about it, and paint about it. "Home" is their true desire!

My friend Allen Shamblin wrote the Grammy Award–winning song "The House That Built Me." Miranda Lambert recorded it. It's a song about an earthly home, and it's also a song about our heavenly home. When we hear the song we think, *If I could just go home; if I could just touch home.* Why? Because somehow we know home heals the brokenness of our hearts and we yearn to go to our eternal home.

In the classic movie *The Wizard of Oz*, Kansas farm girl Dorothy Gale gets caught up in a twister and transported to Oz. Her escapades lead her to uncover the wizard. As Dorothy is about to return to Kansas, her dog, Toto, jumps out of the hot air balloon's basket and Dorothy runs after him. The wizard, unable to control the balloon, leaves without her. As Dorothy despairs of ever getting back home, Glinda appears and tells her that she always had the power to return home, but that she needed to learn for herself that she did not have to run away to find her heart's desire. Dorothy bids her friends good-bye, then follows Glinda's instructions to close her eyes, tap her heels together three times, and keep repeating, "There's no place like home."

While the movie is fantasy, it does highlight our insatiable hunger to return home. There is something about home, and every one of us has that inner desire and longing to go there. There's also something about heaven, and everyone, deep inside of them, has a longing to go there.

Many of us are on that journey. Our destination is heaven. Not only do we have a longing for that place, but God is preparing it for His beloved. Here's something beautiful to remember: As much as we can't wait to get there, He can't wait for us to come home.

The psalmist writes in Psalm 116:15, "Precious in the sight of the Lord is the death of His saints." The Hebrew word for *precious* means "valuable." We are valuable to Him. This too goes back to Eden. God walked the garden with Adam. There is something that happens when we enter into God's presence and see Him face-to-face, eye-to-eye. What parent doesn't love it when a child comes home? God feels the same way when we come home.

Eternity is in our hearts. It's been there since the Garden of Eden. We sing about it, we write about it, and God can't wait for us to get there.

Our Heavenly Citizenship

C. S. Lewis wrote, "If I find in myself a desire which no experience in this world can satisfy, the most probable explanation is that I was made for another world."[2]

Quite simply, we not only long to be in heaven, we were made for it. That was God's original intent and design. This fallen world is only a temporary place. With all of its corrupt and decaying ways, it's not our home.

Therefore, our hearts should not be captured by what the world has to offer. We should not be deceived by its ways or discouraged by its troubles. We should not let it get the best of us because we are not meant to stay here. We as believers are going to another place. We live by a different set of values than the world's; we're not of this world.

Paul wrote in Philippians 3:20, "Our citizenship is in heaven, from which we also eagerly wait for the Savior, the Lord Jesus Christ." Why do we eagerly await Jesus Christ's return? Because we realize our citizenship is not here. Mother Teresa said, "People ask me about death and whether I look forward to it and I answer, 'Of course, because I am going home!'"[3]

In John 14:1–3 Jesus says,

> Let not your heart be troubled; you believe in God, believe also in Me. In My Father's house are many mansions; if it were not so, I would have told you. I go to prepare a place for you. And if I go and prepare a place for you, I will come again and receive you to Myself; that where I am, there you may be also.

He's saying, "Saints, don't let this world trouble you. Don't let it drag you down to despair. It's not your eternal home. It doesn't have the final word over you. As hard and rough as the world might be, whatever hardship you are facing, don't let your heart be troubled."

If you are a believer, Jesus is personally and lovingly building your eternal dwelling place right now.

There are not many more personal, warm, enduring, and intimate things than that simple four-letter word—home. It's wonderful, and it becomes even more so when Jesus says, "I'm going to prepare your eternal home, right now." Have you ever thought about that? If you are a believer, Jesus is personally and lovingly building your eternal dwelling place right now.

Now that I have you thinking about that, have you ever wondered what He's using for building materials and supplies? He's building with whatever it is you're sowing into the future. He's using every eternal seed you've ever sown. Every bit of work that your hand produces in the harvest and every bit of reward that comes as a result—those are the building blocks He's using for your future heavenly home. We, as believers and followers of Jesus Christ, have a dwelling there waiting for us that's built by Jesus Himself. It makes perfect sense that we should prepare our hearts and get them in the right focus now for what is being prepared for us to enjoy later, when we graduate from this world to eternity.

Heavenly Home Perspective

We've learned much from Jesus, Paul, and a few others about the issue of heaven being our real home, and thus becoming our perspective. Looking at a couple more key individuals in Scripture will deepen our understanding. Both Peter and Abraham realized the importance of having a heavenly perspective and life focus. They knew heaven was their real home.

Peter's Perspective

Peter wrote in 1 Peter 1:1, "Peter, an apostle of Jesus Christ, to the pilgrims of the Dispersion in Pontus, Galatia, Cappadocia, Asia, and Bithynia."

He's calling believers in Jesus Christ "pilgrims." He has a very pointed purpose for using that word—he wanted them to understand the mind-set needed while still in this world. We as believers are not earth-dwellers; we are pilgrims. We are a people who are not in their real home.

This perspective is still on Peter's heart as he continues to write. In 1 Peter 2:11 we read, "Beloved, I beg you as sojourners and pilgrims, abstain from fleshly lusts which war against the soul."

Again, he calls them "sojourners and pilgrims."

What is a pilgrim? *The Complete Word Study Dictionary* defines a *pilgrim* as "a stranger, not simply one who is passing through, but a foreigner who has settled down, however briefly, next to or among native people."[4] It defines *sojourner*, which is sometimes translated "stranger," as "one who dwells in a foreign country, a temporary dweller not having a settled habitation in the place where he currently resides."[5] A sojourner is a person who has a home that is near, but it's not right here.

Peter's perspective for believers was that, like pilgrims and sojourners, they were away from their true home. He felt this world was a temporary stopover and ultimately not worth living for. The world's fading, decaying, corruptible ways and treasures have little eternal value.

Jonathan Edmonson, a respected Methodist preacher from the mid-1800s, shared Peter's perspective and wrote, "We are strangers and pilgrims on earth—but we look forward to heaven as our Eternal home."[6]

Scripture calls us strangers, sojourners, and pilgrims. We're called to be eternally minded believers who know in our hearts that heaven is our real home. And that's what should captivate us, not this earth.

Abraham's Perspective

To understand this great patriarch's heavenly perspective fully, we have to read what's recorded in the New Testament about him. Hebrews 11:9–10, 13–16 tells us:

> By faith he dwelt in the land of promise as in a foreign country, dwelling in tents with Isaac and Jacob, the heirs with him of the same promise; for he waited for the city which has foundations,

whose builder and maker is God. . . . These all died in faith, not having received the promises, but having seen them afar off were assured of them, embraced them and confessed that they were strangers and pilgrims on the earth. For those who say such things declare plainly that they seek a homeland. And truly if they had called to mind that country from which they had come out, they would have had opportunity to return. But now they desire a better, that is, a heavenly country. Therefore, God is not ashamed to be called their God, for He has prepared a city for them.

ABRAHAM SOJOURNED IN A FOREIGN COUNTRY

Verse 9 tells us that Abraham sojourned in the land of promise as a stranger in a foreign country. He wasn't too settled into God's blessing. He was looking heavenward.

Abraham was wealthy. He had abundance. Yet despite all of his wealth, the blessing of God didn't take him away from the God of blessing. He wasn't so settled into this world, having the land-of-promise perspective, that he took his eye from the promise of heaven.

I'm fortunate to live in a beautiful place. Williamson County in Tennessee, with its rolling hills, green grass, and horses, can be breathtaking and a lot of fun when you like the outdoors

We're sojourners and heaven is our real home.

as our family does. We used to live in Southern California and we often go back for a vacation. The ocean and the mountains are beautiful to behold and enjoy. Yet with all that beauty, we can't become too attached to this world. We're sojourners just like Abraham. We're not going to be here very long. When He calls us home we can't have our fists clenched around the things of this world. Our hands need to hold the things of this world loosely. We're sojourners and heaven is our real home.

Abraham was a traveler. He wasn't tied down or tethered to this world. He saw himself as a stranger just as Peter and Paul did.

ABRAHAM WAITED FOR GOD'S BEST

Verse 10 tells us that Abraham waited (the Greek word can be translated "to wait in confident expectancy") for a city with foundations (meaning "substance"). He was on the lookout for something with real, solid, eternal staying power that was built by God.

Abraham wasn't going to wait for just any builder. He waited for God's best. Abraham never lived in a house made out of brick or stone. He lived his life in a tent because he was looking for this city, this eternal place called heaven. Abraham sojourned and he waited expectantly for what God had for him. Abraham refused to let the things of this world capture his heart—his heart was secure in heaven.

ABRAHAM SAW GOD'S PROMISE

While it was far off in the distance, Abraham still saw God's promise (verse 13). When we want to see something that is far away from us, most of us need to look intently. We may squint our eyes a bit, trying to focus and stare until we find it. As far off as heaven may have been, Abraham saw it. He believed it was just over the horizon, and his squinting eyes and wrinkling face were intent to stay focused on it. He was assured of it.

Seeing the promise changed how Abraham made decisions. All we have to do is read Genesis 13 to see how heaven's promise guided him. He was with his nephew, Lot, and they found themselves in a challenging situation. There was not enough land for all their sheep. There was Abraham, blessed, older, and with great stature. What did he do? He told Lot essentially,

"Take the land that you want. Whatever you choose, I'll choose what remains. If you go this way, I'll go that way." This great man chose humility and peace over pride and arrogance. He showed grace. He saw the promise, and because his heart was in heaven, he made his decisions with that perspective as his filter.

Seeing the promise also caused Abraham to confess that he was a stranger and pilgrim here on this earth. Abraham wasn't going to settle into the temporary, fading, corruptible glory of this world. His heart wasn't here. He knew he was just passing through earth to get to his heavenly home.

A heavenly perspective has forever changed my heart. Now my struggle is how to help you see the importance of that perspective.

How can I beg you to abstain from the earthly lusts and the pride of life that come with a worldly citizenship? How can I instill in you a value system contrary to that of your earthly home? The only way I can is to help you see that you are a pilgrim and a sojourner. You were not made for this place; you were made for heaven. While you are on this earth, see it in the distance and have that perspective.

English writer and scholar Augustus William Hare wrote, "Above all, we know that heaven is our home, the place we ought to be journeying, the city of our destination."[7]

Abraham Yearned for His Homeland

We see in verse 14 that those who have this heavenly perspective seek a homeland. The Greek word used is sometimes translated as "country." It means "one's own country, the place where one's father or ancestors lived, fatherland, native country."[8] When we have a heavenly perspective, we take a stand and people can see it. It's obvious that our hearts are not here; they're yearning to be in the place of our Father—our Fatherland.

ABRAHAM DIDN'T LOOK BACK

Abraham didn't look back to the Ur of the Chaldeans, the land of his birth. He didn't look down to the Promised Land, the land of milk and honey. As great and wonderful as it was, Abraham knew it didn't compare to what God was preparing for him. He set his sights onward and upward.

You were not made for this place; you were made for heaven.

Paul, like Abraham and Peter, is writing about our perspective. Instead of spending our time on earth looking back or looking down, we need to look forward to heaven and up to Jesus. We need to put this world behind us and not look back in regret, shame, or want. We need to spend our time as pilgrims keeping our minds set on heaven and operating in the mind of Christ.

We have to let eternity capture our hearts. Randy Alcorn wrote

> To long for Christ is to long for Heaven, for that is where we will be with him. God's people are "longing for a better country" (Hebrews 11:16). We cannot set our eyes on Heaven without setting our eyes on Christ. Still, it is not only Christ but "things above" we are to set our minds on.[9]

Abraham and all of the saints listed in this section of Hebrews were stretched out and reaching for a heavenly country. They wanted heaven and the God of heaven. The writer goes on: "Therefore God is not ashamed to be called their God" (11:16). The desire and passion these people of faith showed God was matched by His affirmation and blessing. He's building a special mansion for each one of us in a special place. It's a place we need to desire deeply in our hearts. It's our true eternal home.

Welcome Home

Paul wrote in Ephesians 2:19, "You are no longer strangers and foreigners, but fellow citizens with the saints and members of the household of God."

God wants us to see our lives through the lens of being strangers, sojourners, pilgrims, and foreigners on this earth. Simultaneously, He wants us to know that we are not strangers, pilgrims, and foreigners in the household of God. There, we are fellow citizens. That is where we belong.

Our time on this earth is but a blink of an eye compared to the eternity we will be spending with God in heaven.

Heaven is our real home. Our time on this earth is but a blink of an eye compared to the eternity we will be spending with God in heaven. Let's change the way we are living and walk on earth with a heavenly perspective.

4

Heaven Is Our Real Hope

Human Hope vs. Real Hope

Quite often people define hope as a wish for something good to happen. It's a longing for something to come true. We hope our kids get good grades, we hope our team wins, or we hope that our car can last one more year. Hope is a desire that our lives will get better.

There's nothing wrong with a positive outlook, but there is something wrong with optimism that is from the world's viewpoint. It's not true hope; it's based on what people can achieve or what a certain set of conditions produce. It's based on people or institutions, and they don't last. That's human hope.

Real hope is deeply rooted in God and a heavenly perspective. We can have hope in Him because He's unshakable, unchangeable, and eternal. The apostle John shared what Jesus said about this in John 10:27–30:

My sheep hear My voice, and I know them, and they follow Me. And I give them eternal life, and they shall never perish; neither shall anyone snatch them out of My hand. My Father, who has given them to Me, is greater than all; and no one is able to snatch them out of My Father's hand. I and My Father are one.

Hope that is rooted in Him cannot be taken from us. We're secure in His hand and we can enjoy a home with Him in heaven forever. This is our godly hope.

As we develop a heart for heaven, we come to realize that this is our real hope. When heaven is the source of our hope, that hope will encourage, steady, and direct us as we live here. It must be something that is always before us. E. M. Bounds wrote, "The heaven of fact exists all glorious and enduring, but this fact of heaven must enter our experience, and then of this experience hope is born."[1] He's saying that as heaven becomes our focus and perspective, real hope is born. The more we gaze at heaven, the more hope we will have.

In this chapter we're going deeper into heaven's hope and how we can have greater hope as a result of gazing long and hard upon heaven.

Living Hope

The apostle Peter wrote in 1 Peter 1:3–4,

> Blessed be the God and Father of our Lord Jesus Christ, who according to His abundant mercy has begotten us again to a living hope through the resurrection of Jesus Christ from the dead, to an inheritance incorruptible and undefiled and that does not fade away, reserved in heaven for you.

Peter reminds us that because of Jesus' resurrection, we have a living hope of experiencing a resurrected life in heaven. It comes with a great inheritance that is incorruptible, undefiled, and unfading, and it's reserved just for us!

The more we gaze at heaven, the more hope we will have.

These words are extremely important as we gain a deeper understanding of heaven's real hope.

Incorruptible

The Greek word used here is the same word Paul uses in Romans 1:23 to describe God. It literally means "exempt from wear, waste, and final perishing."[2] It's something that will never decay or wither away. There is nothing about our heavenly inheritance that withers, wears, or shrinks.

Undefiled

This means "unpolluted, unstained, unsoiled, undefiled by sin, sincere, unalloyed, and holy as being free from evil."[3] There is no residue of the curse in our heavenly inheritance. With all the absolute yuck we're faced with in the world today, isn't it good to know that all of that will be completely absent from our inheritance in heaven?

Unfading

Our heavenly inheritance is not something beautiful that lasts only for a while and then fades. *The Complete Word Study Dictionary* says, "It is of unfailing loveliness, reserved for the faithful in heaven."[4] Our inheritance is perpetual. It will never stop astounding us. Heaven and all that it is will never grow old. There will always be newness and freshness, and nothing will fade away.

Richard Carpenter wrote this in the 1600s:

> In God we shall have riches without care, honor without fear, beauty without fading, joy without sorrow, contentment without vexation, and all good things, not one after one but all together; and without the defects annexed to them in this imperfect world.[5]

Reserved

This means "particularly to watch, observe attentively, keep the eyes fixed upon. Figuratively, to obey, observe, fulfill a duty, precept, law or custom, to vigilantly watch."[6] God is diligently and vigilantly watching over our heavenly inheritance. His eye is fixed upon it for us. The Almighty is guarding our eternal future.

We have a living hope that is far greater than any hope that we can find on this earth.

Peter continues just a few verses later in 1 Peter 1:13, "Therefore gird up the loins of your mind, be sober, and rest your hope fully upon the grace that is to be brought to you at the revelation of Jesus Christ."

He starts with "therefore." It brings together these four incredible words: *incorruptible, undefiled, unfading,* and *reserved.* Then He challenges us to get our heads—our thinking and our sight—right by being sober. He's serious about this. He says, "Rest totally on the living hope of Jesus. Rest yourself fully in the grace of heaven that you are going to experience."

We have this incredible inheritance that is guarded by God, and that should give us tremendous hope. It's not going anywhere; it's reserved for us. We should rest on the hope of this

70

inheritance, not in the circumstances of this world. We can't rest our hope in our bank account or our jobs. They don't pass the test—they are not incorruptible, undefiled, unfading, and reserved. If you rest your hope on anything of this world, you will be disappointed!

When we rest ourselves on this living hope, suddenly we're more heavenly minded. No matter how crazy things get here on this little planet, we have a better, living hope. We have joy in that hope, and that hope anchors our souls. Our living hope is in heaven.

Hope for Healing and Freedom

Peter gives us a tremendous glimpse of heaven and the hope we have there. Let's not just glimpse at heaven; let's fully gaze upon it and the hope it brings.

Oftentimes we can better understand something if we know what it is *not*. For example, the guessing game of Twenty Questions is a popular way to understand what something is by knowing what it *is not*.

We are going to gain a deeper understanding of heaven by looking at things that are *not* there. Their absence will make heaven incredibly awesome.

Learning that these things won't be in heaven is some of the best news we could ever hear, and it also helps us see its magnificence even more clearly. This list helps us not to be apprehensive about going there. Rather, it gives us hope and a longing for the things above. We want to experience heaven because we'll be free of so much of what we have to endure on earth. It's incredibly exciting, and it's in that hope that we can find rest and peace.

71

Scripture	What Is *Not* in heaven
Revelation 20:10	The devil and his demons are not in heaven. Satan's deceptive works are not there.
Revelation 21:4	There will be no tears in heaven. God will wipe away every one of them. There will be no death, pain, or sorrow.
Revelation 21:8	Murder, sexual immorality, pornography, sorcery, drug addiction, and witchcraft are not in heaven. Every evil thing that these sins create is completely gone and absent from heaven.
Revelation 21:23–25	There's no darkness in heaven. God illuminates heaven with His glory.
Revelation 21:27	There is no sin in heaven. Nothing enters heaven that will defile, contaminate, or pollute it. Nothing is in heaven that doesn't reflect the perfection of God.
Revelation 22:3	There's no more curse in heaven. Think about it. Every byproduct of the fall is nonexistent.

Hope for Beauty and Glory

We have a living hope of heaven because of this incredible inheritance that is incorruptible, undefiled, unfading, and reserved for us.

We have a magnificent hope because of all the terrible things of this earth that are *not* in heaven.

We also have a glorious hope because of all the wonderful things that *are* in heaven.

Before we get to this list, however, we need to make sure we're not simply using our own preconceived ideas. Many of us have a natural bent to minimize. We look at something through the lens of our own experience, knowledge, and imagination, and if we can't picture something being the way it is, we minimize it.

When we're contemplating the glorious hope of heaven, we dare not minimize its majesty.

Robert Hall, a pastor and author from the 1700s, understood this and wrote, "In the contemplation of God, we are in no danger of going beyond our Subject; we are conversing about an infinite being. In the depths of Whose essence and purposes we are forever lost."[7]

There will be no tears in heaven. God will wipe away every one of them.

He's pointing out that when we talk about God and the things of God, our finite minds can't have thoughts that are greater than God really is. What awaits us in heaven is actually beyond description. There's no danger that we will think too grand a thought about eternity.

So as you read the list below of *what is* in heaven, don't minimize it. Let God and His Spirit guide you to think with a sanctified imagination within the confines of biblical truth.

Our glorious hope starts with what Paul wrote in 1 Corinthians 13:12. He said, "Now we see in a mirror, dimly, but then face to face. Now I know in part, but then I shall know just as I also am known."

Right now, living on this earth, we see God dimly, but we are going to see God face-to-face. The dim vision of God we have now, as exhilarating as it can be at times, is just a small drop in the ocean compared to seeing God face-to-face in the glory of heaven.

I love what Bishop Patrick wrote in the 1600s about seeing God:

Seeing God in His glory when we are strengthened to bear it will be a perpetual source of bliss. Then all the attributes of God will shine forth and we shall see the beauty of His holiness, the splendor and brightness of His understanding; the largeness of

His love; His uncorrupted justice; His unexhausted goodness; His immovable truth; His uncontrollable power; His vast dominions, which yet He fills with His presence and administers their affairs with ease, and is magnified and praised in them by the throng of all of His creatures.[8]

In heaven we are going to see God face-to-face and it is going to be mind-blowing.

Paul goes on to say that we're going to know things even as we're known. Here's a question for you: How well are you known? It's probably safe to say that God knows you completely. Consequently, if we are going to know things even as we are known, that means to me that I'm going to know things completely—just as God knows me completely. Can you imagine what that is going to be like?

Our heavenly bodies will have capabilities far beyond anything we can imagine.

Legendary singer and songwriter Eric Clapton, along with Will Jennings, wrote a song called "Tears in Heaven." It came out of Clapton's intense pain following the tragic accidental death of his four-year-old son, Conor. It's one of Clapton's most successful and personal songs as he questions whether or not his son will recognize him in heaven.

The answer to his question is yes—we are going to know people in heaven. Not just relatives and friends, but people we've never met, because we'll all know, even as we are known (1 Corinthians 13:12).

This is part of the mystery and majesty of what heaven is, and there's more.

These are just a few things that are going to make heaven so glorious. We can't even imagine how awesome it's going to be. Do you see why it is our hope and why our perspective needs to be shaped by this wonderful, mysterious, glorious place?

74

Scripture	What *Is* in Heaven
Matthew 8:11 and Luke 12:37	We will have fellowship and communion with both old friends and new.
1 Corinthians 13:12	We will see God face-to-face. We will know, even as we are known. We will know things completely, because we are completely known by God.
Philippians 3:20–21	Our resurrected bodies will be transformed to be like Jesus' glorious body. How fun will that be?
2 Timothy 4:8 and Revelation 2:10	We will have crowns—the crown of righteousness for loving His appearing and the crown of life for being faithful until death. All is recognized, remembered, and rewarded in heaven.
1 John 3:2	To see God, we'll need to be like Him, and we cannot do that in our current, corrupt bodies. Our heavenly bodies will have capabilities far beyond anything we can imagine.
Revelation 3:12	We will be pillars in God's temple. A pillar represents strength, security, and stability. We will be rock solid in our relationship with God.
Revelation 21:7	We will inherit all things from the Creator of the universe through our intimate Father/child relationship with Him. Can you imagine the inheritance from almighty God?
Revelation 22:1–2	There will be water of life, a tree of life, and healing leaves for God's people to experience. Life and healing will abound.
Revelation 22:5	We will rule and reign forever as kings and priests to our God. We will serve and worship Him without hindrance, obstacle, or hassle—forever.
Revelation 22:12	We will have rewards. We'll be rewarded according to our works. Remember, every Kingdom-expanding act is remembered and rewarded in heaven.

Your Real Hope (and Home)

In the last two chapters we took a look at heaven. We studied Scriptures that show us that heaven, not this earth or the

75

things of this earth, is our real hope and our real home. We're pilgrims—not residents—on this earth.

All of this makes sense if you are a believer in Jesus Christ. But what if you are not? What if you're reading this book and you're not sure about your relationship with Jesus, or you're not absolutely certain that you are going to be with Him in heaven?

Before we go any further, let me help you make a decision that will last for an eternity.

Way too often we don't stop long enough to think about what really matters. We lose focus on our true home and our true hope. We're so busy that we don't ask, "What about God, and what about eternity?" In the next few pages, we're going to answer that question with some of God's facts. I'm going to present His facts and then ask you to make the most important decision of your life.

Making a Decision

God wants you to know Him and experience His amazing love for you, but before that can happen, you must make a decision. Most of the time we don't like to make serious decisions. In our society, being lukewarm is comfortable and popular. In this middle ground, everyone's okay and no one has to take a stand or make bold commitments. Lukewarm choices are usually based on personal pleasure and popular opinion, rarely on God's truth.

That's why God commands us to live boldly. He beckons us out of the lukewarm middle where we're undecided. Jesus said, "He who is not with Me is against Me, and he who does not gather with Me scatters abroad" (Matthew 12:30). He's very clear. Jesus cuts through people's opinions and asks you to make a decision. There is no such thing as a closet Christian.

Fact #1: Death Is Inevitable

King David wrote in Psalm 39:5, "Indeed, You have made my days as handbreadths, and my age is as nothing before You; certainly every man at his best state is but vapor." David referred to handbreadths, which is just the width of the palm of your hand. He described life as a vapor, meaning something that passes quickly. Our lives, in God's eyes, are no wider than the palm of our hands and pass very quickly like a vapor. Death is inevitable. We're not invincible.

James wrote in the New Testament, "You do not know what will happen tomorrow. For what is your life? It is even a vapor that appears for a little time and then vanishes away" (James 4:14). We don't know what will happen tomorrow, or even in the next moment. Therefore, we must be prepared today. Sarah and I have peace, comfort, and hope that comes from the fact that our son Josiah made the bold decision to trust Christ as his Savior, so he was ready to meet Jesus. Jesus has given him eternal life.

Have you prepared for your own mortality? You must make a decision in advance, because it's too late to make it after your death.

Fact #2: Heaven Isn't Automatic

Heaven isn't everyone's default destination, contrary to popular opinion. When death happens, we like to say, "That person is in a better place" . . . but are we really sure?

The absolute truth must come from God's Word, not people's opinions.

The apostle Paul wrote in the New Testament in Galatians 5:19–21:

The works of the flesh are evident, which are: adultery, fornication, uncleanness, lewdness, idolatry, sorcery, hatred, contentions, jealousies, outbursts of wrath, selfish ambitions, dissensions, heresies, envy, murders, drunkenness, revelries, and the like; of which I tell you beforehand, just as I also told you in time past, that those who practice such things will not inherit the kingdom of God.

Paul is saying that you cannot live a life of sin, rejecting Christ and His solution for your sin, and then expect to spend eternity in the Kingdom of God. It simply doesn't work that way.

We all must prepare for eternity by saying yes to Christ and living a life that reflects that decision. There are no guarantees without making that decision.

It is clear from God's Word that sinfulness and sinners will never enter heaven. Only those written in the Lamb's Book of Life (people who have said yes to Jesus) will be granted access.

Fact #3: Hell Is Real

Jesus talked more about hell than all the other prophets combined. It was an important topic to Him; He wanted people to know the consequences of their decisions. In Luke 16:19–31 Jesus talked about a poor man, Lazarus, who went to heaven, and a rich man who went to hell. The story was contrary to traditional Jewish thinking. Most listeners would have thought, *Isn't it obvious that the rich man would automatically go to heaven?* Jesus tells us that the rich man was "in torments in Hades."

Hell is a literal place of torment for those who consciously and willingly reject the matchless, sacrificial love of God found in Jesus Christ. Hell is not a state of being, it's not a metaphor, it's not a symbol. Hell is a real place. The people who are in hell are in torment because they could have said yes, but they said no to God's free gift of eternal life for their entire lives.

It's too late to make the decision when you're in hell. You must cry out for God's love and mercy on this side of eternity.

C. S. Lewis put it this way: "A man can't be *taken* to hell, or *sent* to hell: you can only get there on your own steam."[9] In order to go to hell, you have to walk over the sacrificial love that Jesus poured out for us on the cross. You have to willingly say no to God's salvation, and guess what? His salvation is the one thing that can keep you out of hell. Listen, when someone ends up in hell, it is God giving them for all eternity exactly what they wanted—a life without God and His goodness . . . forever.

Fact #4: God Loves You

Yes, God loves *you*, with all your sin and baggage and wounds and addictions and doubts. Yes, *you*, with all your stuff . . . God loves *you*! He loves you in spite of all you've done.

You need Him, He knows it, and that's why God sent Jesus. He knows everything about you, and His greatest desire is to take your sinfulness and brokenness, and love you into a place of healing and redemption. God says, "When life on this earth is over, I want to love you for all eternity in heaven, where there is no more sin, suffering, or brokenness."

Romans 5:8 says, "God demonstrates His own love toward us, *in that while we were still sinners, Christ died for us*" (emphasis mine).

> *Yes, God loves you, with all your sin and baggage and wounds and addictions and doubts.*

God loves you so much that He didn't even wait for you to clean up your act before He sent Jesus to take the penalty of your sin and die in your place. God didn't just talk about love—He demonstrated it. God's demonstrated love hung on a cross for *you*—and He did it while you hated and rejected Him. Now, that's love! It's love in action, not a philosophy.

So what are you waiting for? It doesn't matter what you've done in the past—let it be your past and start a new life in Christ today. God loves you so much that He sent Jesus to die for you while you were still a sinner. God loves you so much that He's waiting for you, in your true home, and He offers you true and eternal hope.

Fact #5: You Must Be Born Again

It's not about religion—it's about new birth. John 3 records Jesus' conversation about eternal life with a very religious man named Nicodemus. He said this: "Most assuredly, I say to you, unless one is born again, he cannot see the kingdom of God. . . . Do not marvel that I said to you, 'You must be born again'" (vv. 3, 7).

Nicodemus was a good man; he lived a "religious" life. He tried hard to keep the Ten Commandments, yet he fell short, like all of us do. Jesus essentially told him, "It's not about religion—it's about being born again in order to live in the Kingdom of God forever."

You must be born again. It's not a bumper sticker or just a saying. It's reality, and it's necessary so that you can have an abundant life on earth and eternal life in heaven.

HOW TO BE BORN AGAIN

Jesus said in the gospel of Mark, "The time is fulfilled, and the kingdom of God is at hand. Repent, and believe in the gospel" (1:15).

Repent. To repent means to change your mind and change your direction, to quit running from God and run toward God instead. Acts 17:30 says, "Truly, these times of ignorance God overlooked, but now commands all men everywhere to repent." You must repent.

Believe in the gospel. Believe Jesus rose from the dead. Believe the Good News that Jesus came to pay the price for all of your sins (past, present, and future). Believe and trust that Jesus died in your place because God loves you.

Receive Christ. John 1:12 says, "As many as received Him, to them He gave the right to become children of God, to those who believe in His name." Receiving Christ is something you do as an act of your own will through prayer.

YOUR PRAYER OF DECISION

If you are ready to make this decision for Christ, simply tell Him. Tell Him you want to repent. Tell Him you want to turn away from your past and run to Him. Tell Him you believe in the gospel—you know Jesus paid the price for your sins and you believe in Him. Receive Jesus. Invite Him into every part of your life to heal you, to restore you, to break your bondage to sin, and to open your heart to His love and gift of eternal life.

If you are ready to make this decision for Christ, simply tell Him.

It's that simple. Your prayer may sound something like this:

Heavenly Father, I repent. I turn to you now. I realize I can't get to heaven on my own. I believe Jesus Christ took the penalty of my sin and died on the cross in my place so I could know you, love you, and spend eternity with you in heaven. I believe Jesus rose from the dead, and I receive Him now as my Lord and Savior. Thank you for accepting me into your eternal family. Amen.

If you prayed that prayer, celebrate! You are a new creation in the family of God. Angels and saints in heaven are rejoicing because you are now a part of God's family. Remember this day—it's special. You have been born again. New life is yours. Salvation, forgiveness, peace with God, your eternal home, and hope . . . it's all yours. Congratulations! You just made the best decision of your life. You have a new home and a new hope in heaven.

5

A Glimpse of Heaven

Not Even Close

Let me say something that might sound a little outrageous to you—our best days on this earth don't even come close to comparing to our days in heaven. When we realize this truth it should do two things for us: First, it should help us loosen our grip on our earthly life and all the things this world has to offer. Second, it should cause us to long for heaven and all that Jesus has prepared for us (John 14:2–3). The truth of the matter is, we live in a fallen world, and as beautiful, fun, and enjoyable as this life can be, it doesn't compare to the glory yet to be revealed (Romans 8:18). In the next few pages I want to give you a glimpse of heaven. I want to help you see its glory directly from God's Word. I'll be honest; I'm teasing you for a purpose. I'm whetting your appetite so you'll desperately desire all of its benefits. Why? So the God of heaven and the heaven of God can be your purpose and passion. Get ready for an adventure.

The New Heaven and the New Earth

We need to start at the end. We need to look at the apostle John's vision from the end of the book of Revelation. So let's look at the new heaven and make that our focal point. John wrote:

> Now I saw a new heaven and a new earth, for the first heaven and the first earth had passed away. Also there was no more sea. Then I, John, saw the holy city, New Jerusalem, coming down out of heaven from God, prepared as a bride adorned for her husband. And I heard a loud voice from heaven saying, "Behold, the tabernacle of God is with men, and He will dwell with them, and they shall be His people. God Himself will be with them and be their God. And God will wipe away every tear from their eyes; there shall be no more death, nor sorrow, nor crying. There shall be no more pain, for the former things have passed away."
>
> Then He who sat on the throne said, "Behold, I make all things new." And He said to me, "Write, for these words are true and faithful."
>
> Revelation 21:1–5

Does this sound familiar? It should sound a lot like the Garden of Eden. John is describing a new heaven and a new earth, and just as in Eden, God is dwelling among His people. Remember, God walked in the garden in the cool of the day (Genesis 3:8). God Himself was with Adam and Eve.

Also note what else John says. In the new heaven there will be no tears, no death, no sorrow, no crying, no pain, and no corruption of any kind. That sounds like Eden to me as well.

John tells us that it will be *new*. The word John uses implies better because it's so different. It speaks of something that has been renewed, and therefore something superior and more splendid than anything we've ever seen. Our God does things like that.

84

He's not a stingy, reluctant giver. He's extravagant and limitless, and He has a surprise for us at every turn. That's who God is and how glorious the new heaven will be.

I have a theory. I think how we see God radically affects how we see heaven. If we see God in our own self-designed box, full of laws and restrictions, then we'll see anything He creates, heaven included, from a sterile, pre-dictable, and boring mind-set. However, if we see God as a loving, generous Father who wants all the best for His children, then we will see heaven from an open and imaginative perspective, and that gives us hope, encouragement, and such excitement that we can't wait to see what He has planned.

Our best days on this earth don't even come close to comparing to our days in heaven.

Better Than the Garden

John continues his picture in Revelation 21:18–21:

> The construction of its wall was of jasper; and the city was pure gold, like clear glass. The foundations of the wall of the city were adorned with all kinds of precious stones: the first foundation was jasper, the second sapphire, the third chalcedony, the fourth emerald, the fifth sardonyx, the sixth sardius, the seventh chrysolite, the eighth beryl, the ninth topaz, the tenth chrysoprase, the eleventh jacinth, and the twelfth amethyst. The twelve gates were twelve pearls: each individual gate was of one pearl. And the street of the city was pure gold, like transparent glass.

Can you imagine streets made of pure gold? Materials and things we think are precious will be common building materials in heaven. The opulence of the new heaven will far exceed any city of this world. In heaven, we will walk on these streets just as we walk on asphalt today. The Garden of Eden had gold, but not gold that was so pure it was like glass. Heaven's walls are made of precious stones. Heaven has pearls the size of gates!

John continues his glimpse of heaven and writes in Revelation 21:23, "The city had no need of the sun or of the moon to shine in it, for the glory of God illuminated it. The Lamb *is* its light." Adam and Eve needed the moon and sun for light. We won't in heaven because God's glory will emit enough light for us to clearly see everything. Rebecca Springer wrote, "The air was soft and balmy, though invigorating; and instead of sunlight there was a golden and rosy glory everywhere, something like the afterglow of a Southern sunset in midsummer."[1] There is no need for light in heaven, for God is its light!

> *Materials and things we think are precious will be common building materials in heaven.*

Not only is there no need for light, John tells us that we are called and made priests and kings. In Revelation 5:10 and 21:24 we are told that we will rule and reign in the new heaven, much like Adam and Eve were called to have dominion in the Garden. We will be redeemed people who have the ability as kings and priests to reign on earth forever.

John continues to show how the new heaven will be more than the Garden. In Revelation 21:27 and 22:3 he writes, "But there shall by no means enter it anything that defiles, or causes an abomination or a lie. . . . And there shall be no more curse, but the throne of God and of the Lamb shall be in it, and His servants shall serve Him." Remember, before the serpent deceived Eve and she ate the apple, she and Adam lived in a perfect place. There was no sin, no curse, no battles, and no temptations. The same is true for the new heaven. The struggles of the flesh, the battles we fight, the temptations that we ward off, the things we go through to keep renewing our minds and think on heavenly, godly things will be gone—forever. There will be no sin. In fact, there will be no knowledge of sin. Just like Eden before the fall of man, the new heaven will be perfect and without struggle, sin, and Satan.

There's one more comparison. John wrote in Revelation 22:1–2:

> And he showed me a pure river of water of life, clear as crystal, proceeding from the throne of God and of the Lamb. In the middle of its street, and on either side of the river, was the tree of life, which bore twelve fruits, each tree yielding its fruit every month. The leaves of the tree were for the healing of the nations.

Like Eden, there is a river, but this river flows and proceeds from the throne of God. This river is called the very water of life. There is also the tree of life. It's part of the new heaven, but this isn't just any tree: This tree's leaves heal the nations. There are all kinds of questions about what that means. But suffice it to say, that tree has power to heal and give life and is unlike the Tree of Life found in Eden, which only gave life.

In just these few verses, we see what God always intended for us, and we see what's coming our way. We see how Eden before the fall was wonderful, but even in all its beauty and splendor, it didn't compare to heaven.

This picture should, by itself, inspire us to live differently here on earth. As Paul wrote in Colossians 3:1, "Since you have been raised to new life with Christ, set your sights on the realities of heaven, where Christ sits in the place of honor at God's right hand" (NLT).

Professor and writer F. F. Bruce wrote:

[Those who have faith] continue to live on earth in their mortal bodies, but they have embarked on a new way of life. The motive power enabling them to follow this new way of life is imparted by Him from the glory in which He now lives . . . they must pursue those things which belong to the heavenly realm where He reigns.[2]

Both Paul and F. F. Bruce point to fixing our eyes on heaven and all that it has for us. We've briefly glimpsed how heaven is exceedingly better than the Garden of Eden. Let's now look at what it will be like for us.

Heaven Ain't Boring

It's both interesting and dangerous to talk about heaven. When we point out the sinless tranquility and how incredibly beautiful the new heaven and the new earth are going to be, it can lead people to an incorrect opinion that somehow this glorious creation is also a place of eternal apathy and boredom. Or, as John Eldredge says in his book *The Journey of Desire*,

Nearly every Christian I have spoken with has some idea that eternity is an unending church service. . . . We have settled on an image of the never-ending sing-along in the sky, one great hymn after another, forever and ever, amen. And our heart sinks. Forever and ever? That's it? That's the good news? And then we sigh and feel guilty that we are not more "spiritual." We lose heart, and we turn once more to the present to find what life we can.[3]

I can assure you that heaven is not boring and there's no need for you to look at the things of this earth with envy in your heart. How can I speak so boldly? Scripture tells us that heaven, my friends, is everything we can dream it is and more.

People also think heaven is boring because their current spiritual lives are boring. They haven't entered into the thrill of receiving supernatural power to do what God has called them to do—whether that is professional ministry or simply not complaining about the boss at the lunch table. They've never entered the place of risky obedience where you literally do things that you could never do on your own strength.

Our lives in Christ sometimes are boring because we don't know what it's like to completely trust God in the dark night of the soul and to hang on no matter what and say, "God, I refuse to be silenced. I'm not willing to relinquish my worship to circumstance." Suddenly, when we hang on, clutching His hand tightly along the way, we start to realize that God didn't intend our life here on earth to be boring, and He sure didn't intend our life in heaven to be boring. Heaven isn't about harps and strumming a lyre on some puffy white cloud wearing some funky white robe forever.

Scripture tells us that heaven, my friends, is everything we can dream it is and more.

Randy Alcorn wrote, "It's difficult to see beyond the horizon of our experience."[4] If we truly want to see heaven while we're living on earth, we have to remove the distorted lens of what we feel, think, and know. All of us have distorted perceptions of who God is, what He can and cannot do, or how good He is. To get a clearer, undistorted picture, we need to start putting together all of the pieces of God's character, nature, love, plan, creativity, and power. Then, as we work on that jigsaw puzzle, heaven starts looking different. It looks incredible. Unbelievable. Why? Because we're not trapped in our own thinking and opinions. Instead, we're looking at heaven through God's lens of who He is and of all that He wants to do for us.

When we do that, heaven isn't boring. I love what author Mark Buchanan wrote: "[Heaven is where] the *ahh!* of deep satisfaction and the *aha!* of delighted surprise meet, and they kiss."[5] That's the heaven I'm looking for. Everything about that heaven aligns perfectly with the God that we serve. It's not boring, predictable, sterile, or stodgy. It's neither cheap nor chintzy. Instead, it's extravagant, loving, creative, and powerful. It's utter satisfaction and utter surprise at the same time.

Sinless Resurrected Bodies

When we fully understand that heaven isn't boring, the next question seems to be, "What will we be doing?" Before we look into that there's one thing we must understand. In heaven we will have sinless, resurrected bodies that will have unbelievable abilities.

Paul writes in 1 Corinthians 15:42–44 that our earthly bodies are created in corruption. We feel that every day, and it's the result of the fall. We are created in dishonor (reproach), weakness, and frailty. I'm speaking of our current, earthbound bodies.

However, our resurrected bodies are raised in immortality—incorruptible. They are raised in glory, honor, and power, with supernatural abilities. Our bodies may look similar in heaven, but they will be vastly different in terms of their abilities. They will be infinitely beyond anything we can imagine.

In Philippians 3:20–21 Paul reminds us that Jesus Christ "will transform our lowly body that it may be conformed to His glorious body." That means everything that Jesus has we will have.

Jesus had the ability to fly (Acts 1:9). His resurrected body had the ability to appear (John 20) and disappear (Luke 24:30–31), and so will ours if we're conformed to His glorious body. Let me tell you, that's not boring, it's supernaturally thrilling.

When we realize that we will have resurrected bodies, then we can look at what we will be doing differently. We won't be confined to what we know about our physical bodies today. We will have new bodies, fully resurrected and conformed to Jesus' body.

6

What Will We Do in Heaven?

In the conditions discussed in the previous chapter—new heaven, new earth, and with new resurrected bodies with new supernatural abilities—what will we do in heaven?

I think there are at least eight things we will do in heaven.

Create

Revelation 5:9 tells us, "And they sang a new song, saying: 'You are worthy to take the scroll, and to open its seals; for You were slain, and have redeemed us to God by Your blood out of every tribe and tongue and people and nation.'"

This verse tells us that we are going to be singing a *new* song. How does something become new? Somebody has to create it. Newness is the result of creativity, and in heaven, with all its splendor and glory, do you think God is going to give us less creativity than we have on earth? Certainly not!

We will be able to do everything from writing, singing, and painting to gardening, worshiping, and dancing free from any fear, sin, judgment, or constraint of time and space. We will be free to be as creative as heavenly possible.

J. R. R. Tolkien, in the conclusion of his poem *Mythopoeia,* asserted his belief that human creativity will be beatified in heaven by its being made perfect. He writes that souls in heaven will "renew from mirrored truth the likeness of the True. . . . Salvation changes not, nor yet destroys, garden nor gardener, children nor their toys."[1] Tolkien's point is that our creativity is not destroyed in heaven but perfected. Without evil, Tolkien believed, our creativity will reach unimaginable splendor.

> *Nothing we've seen on earth will compare to what we'll create in heaven.*

Take a minute and think about this. What if your favorite writer, artist, or singer-songwriter had the amazing ability to write songs, to paint paintings, to write books with a sinless, resurrected body? Picture them doing what they do so well in heaven! I sincerely believe we haven't heard or seen anything yet. Beethoven, Michelangelo, Shakespeare—what do you think they're writing, painting, and playing today in heaven?

Victor Hugo, the nineteenth-century French poet, playwright, novelist, artist, statesman, and author of *Les Miserables* and *The Hunchback of Notre Dame*, said this about the next life:

I feel within me the future life. For half a century I have been translating my thoughts into prose and verse. History, drama, philosophy, romance, tradition, satire, ode and song. All of these things I have tried. But I feel I haven't given utterance to the thousandth part of what lies within me.[2]

Our creativity will soar to wide-open new places and spaces in heaven. Nothing we've seen on earth will compare to what we'll create in heaven.

Hear Music

We will not only create new things, we'll sing new songs.

An 1880s edition of *The Baptist Magazine* put it this way:

> We never see the redeemed in heaven without hearing them; our eyes are never dazzled with the brightness of their glory but our ears are at the same time ravished with the melody of their songs . . . music is fit for heaven. Music is a pattern of everlasting life in heaven because in heaven, as in music, is perfect freedom and perfect pleasure.[3]

Whatever kind of praise and worship music you like today will be amplified, not louder, but extraordinarily enhanced to purely and pointedly praise God. We will hear sounds and words we've never heard before. We'll experience perfect melody and perfect harmony without any restraint. We will be in the most glorious, technologically advanced concert hall ever created with music that comes from the heart and soul of God Himself.

We'll experience music in heaven as never before.

Worship

Revelation 5:9 tells us that those in heaven will be from "every tribe and tongue and people and nation."

Heaven isn't just creativity and music. It's songs we haven't sung before with a crowd of people with whom we've never worshiped. In heaven there will be people from everywhere raising their voices in their own languages, yet making one sound and singing songs praising and worshiping God. Just as mind-blowing as everything else is in heaven, worship will be no different. Personally I think we'll be in these fantastic worship times looking at each other and saying, "Can you believe this?" What will it be like to see angelic hosts in the millions surrounding the redeemed people of God from every tribe, every nation, and every tongue worshiping the Lamb of God who redeemed us from this world? We can't get close to imagining it.

Leland Ryken, James C. Wilhoit, and Tremper Longman, in their book *The Dictionary of Biblical Imagery*, describe it this way:

> The Lamb receives the same worship from the heavenly assembly as does the one on the throne, and the assembly enlarges to include angels "numbering myriads of myriads and thousands and thousands" and then to encompass the entire cosmos as "every creature in heaven and earth and under the earth and in the sea, and all therein" join in heavenly praise (Rev. 5:11, 13 RSV).[4]

John wrote in Revelation 15:3, "They sing the song of Moses, the servant of God, and the song of the Lamb, saying: 'Great and marvelous are Your works, Lord God Almighty! Just and true are Your ways, O King of the saints!" We'll not only be singing new songs as we worship God, but we'll be singing some old ones too.

We're going to remember what God did for us on earth, and from that remembrance He is going to help us create a new song that worships Him. It might sound like an old hymn or the most contemporary praise song, but we'll be worshiping Him with it along with people whom we've never met as well as people who are familiar to us from our past and our families. We'll be singing our new songs eternally, and we'll all be singing to Him in the perfect key.

Laugh

In Luke 6:21 Jesus says, "Blessed are you who hunger now, for you shall be filled. Blessed are you who weep now, for you shall laugh."

One of the greatest heaven quotes I've ever read is this: "Heaven is the compensation for lost earthly privileges."[5] The authors were showing that the ultimate hope of martyrs and persecuted people was heaven, but I think it can speak more broadly to anyone who has suffered and is hurting. Heaven is a place for those who weep today on earth to regain the joy that has been stolen from them.

Isn't it good to know that in the midst of weeping and brokenness and all the grief that we go through now that our God is a God who says, "Hey, I'm going to more than make up for everything. There is going to be laughter in heaven like you can't imagine"? Author and speaker Liz Curtis Higgs wrote,

> *There is going to be laughter in heaven like you can't imagine.*

There won't be money in heaven, nor marrying, nor tears. But there will be worship and music and praise and joy unspeakable. And, I believe, there will be laughter. It was Martin Luther who said, "If you're not allowed to laugh in heaven, I don't want to go there." Since the many Lutherans among us know their fearless founder will be there, we can surmise that laughter probably will be too.[6]

C. S. Lewis wrote, "Joy is the serious business of heaven."[7]

Psalm 16:11 reminds us, "You will show me the path of life; in Your presence is fullness of joy; at Your right hand are pleasures forevermore."

In God's presence there is fullness of joy. Absolutely nothing will be withheld. At God's right hand are "pleasures forevermore." Those are the *aha*s of heaven. Divine surprises wrapped in eternal joy and, yes, laughter.

Interact With the Animal Kingdom

People ask the question, Are there animals in heaven? When we read the Bible, the answer is a resounding yes, and they are some unique animals that have some very distinctive abilities. Isaiah 11:6–9 says,

> The wolf also shall dwell with the lamb, the leopard shall lie down with the young goat, the calf and the young lion and the fatling together; and a little child shall lead them. The cow and the bear shall graze; their young ones shall lie down together; and the lion shall eat straw like the ox. The nursing child shall play by the cobra's hole, and the weaned child shall put his hand in the viper's den. They shall not hurt nor destroy in all My holy mountain, for the earth shall be full of the knowledge of the Lord as the waters cover the sea.

I agree with many Bible scholars that this verse refers to the millennial kingdom here on earth before the new heaven and the new earth are created. However, I would add this question: Are the new heaven and new earth going to be greater or less than the millennial kingdom on earth? They will be infinitely bigger and better. So when we read Isaiah's prophecy that during the thousand-year reign of Christ there will be animals, we can rest assured there are going to be animals in heaven. We'll experience the thrill of being with a lion, but we won't be afraid or feel in danger.

Revelation 4:7 tells us, "The first living creature was like a lion, the second living creature like a calf, the third living creature had a face like a man, and the fourth living creature was like a flying eagle." If we keep reading (vv. 8–10), we realize that these animals are speaking and giving glory, honor, and thanks to God. We also see that the elders respond to what the animals are saying.

Lastly, Revelation 19:11, 14 says,

> Now I saw heaven opened, and behold, a white horse. And He who sat on him was called Faithful and True, and in righteousness He judges and makes war. . . . And the armies in heaven, clothed in fine linen, white and clean, followed Him on white horses.

Are there animals in heaven? We're going to be riding horses and listening to creatures and walking with lions. Evangelist Billy Graham said in 1999, "God will prepare everything for our perfect happiness in heaven, and if it takes my dog being there, I believe he'll be there."[8]

Work

Yes, there's work in heaven.

Revelation 7:15 tells us, "Therefore they are before the throne of God, and serve Him day and night in His temple. And He who sits on the throne will dwell among them." Based on Revelation 7 and Revelation 22, without question, we will keep on serving Him.

We tend to shy away from this idea because we don't exactly know what this "work" is going to look like. Frankly, I can't help thinking that there are jobs to organize, there are plans to execute; there's building and farming and teaching and exploring and creating and artistry. Who knows how we're going to serve Him, but we're told twice by the apostle John in Revelation that we are going to be serving or continuing to serve God.

There is one difference between our current work and work in heaven. In that happy place, our work will be without the opposition and problems that come from serving God here on earth. Our work in heaven will only and always be completely satisfying and fulfilling. I can't wait to work for Jesus—forever. I can't wait to offer back to Him whatever He gives me, with love, and say, "Lord, anything that you've given me—here it is back to you. I want to serve you and love you and worship you for all of eternity."

Reign With Christ

Revelation 5:10 says, "And have made us kings and priests to our God; and we shall reign on the earth." We are not kings and priests in some sort of passive, uninvolved sense. We are kings and priests who have the privilege and opportunity of reigning with Jesus. We'll be able to execute His will in certain situations—we'll have responsibility and authority given to us so that we can oversee what God wants done.

Revelation 2:26 says, "And he who overcomes, and keeps My works until the end, to him I will give power over the nations." Our reward for overcoming in this life is sharing Christ's reign in heaven.

You may ask, "Where does our authority to reign come from?" I believe that our authority in heaven is a result of how faithful we've served God here on earth. It's a function of how well we've done what He's asked us to do. You see, it's service now, authority and responsibility later. If we're not ready to get our hands dirty now and do His work, why should He give us great authority and responsibility in heaven? If we're not ready to put our hand in the harvest here, why should we expect a promotion when we get to heaven?

We'll have responsibility and authority given to us so that we can oversee what God wants done.

People in heaven get everything that God is—forever. He will reward them based on what they did for Him here and now. If you're not willing to serve and help people here, don't expect much responsibility there.

Relate to God Himself

I've saved the best one for last. We've looked at all kinds of interesting aspects and abilities in heaven, but the greatest thing about heaven is God Himself—the great I AM, Creator of the universe, Redeemer of mankind, Savior of the world, Lover of our souls. Our God will be there to have tangible, intimate relationships with His beloved. He is the God of heaven. (In fact, any time I mention heaven in this book, it includes the God of heaven because we cannot separate Him from heaven.) When we get to heaven our faith will truly become sight.

Remember, in Eden God walked and talked with Adam and Eve. Eden's reality is earth's hope and will one day be heaven's ultimate reward. We will be face-to-face with God forever. St. Augustine said,

God Himself, who is the Author of virtue, shall there be its reward; for, as there is nothing greater or better, He has promised Himself. What else was meant by His word through the prophet,

101

"I will be your God, and ye shall be My people"? . . . He shall be the end of our desires who shall be seen without end, loved without cloy, praised without weariness."[9]

Job, the oldest book of the Bible, records this profound statement:

> For I know that my Redeemer lives, and He shall stand at last on the earth; and after my skin is destroyed, this I know, that in my flesh I shall *see God*, whom I shall *see for myself*, and *my eyes shall behold*, and not another. How my heart yearns within me!
>
> Job 19:25–27, emphasis mine

Job knows God lives and that God will return and reign. He knows that after his earthly body dies, he will receive a new body and that he will personally see God.

God's gift of Himself to us in heaven could not be clearer. Revelation 21:3 says, "And I heard a loud voice from heaven saying, 'Behold, the tabernacle of God is with men, and He will dwell with them, and they shall be His people. God Himself will be with them and be their God.'"

The greatest thing about heaven is God Himself.

God is communicating with a loud voice. He will be with us in heaven.

Revelation 22:3–4 says, "And there shall be no more curse, but the throne of God and of the Lamb shall be in it, and His servants shall serve Him. *They shall see His face*, and His name shall be on their foreheads" (emphasis mine).

Remember in Exodus 33 Moses wanted to see God's glory, and God said, "You cannot see My face; for no man can see my face and live." In heaven, what could not happen in our earthly mortality happens in our immortality! We see God's face and He is with us.

Longing and Preparing for Heaven

Heaven is going to be an incredible place, and when we realize it in our hearts, we'll be as torn as Paul was between heaven and earth.

Psalm 84:1–2 says, "How lovely is Your tabernacle, O Lord of hosts! My soul longs, yes, even faints for the courts of the Lord; my heart and my flesh cry out for the living God."

The more I know about heaven, the more I want to interpret this psalm literally—God's dwelling place is lovely, my soul longs and faints for it, *my heart and flesh cry out for God Himself*!

Charles H. Spurgeon said it best: "*My soul longeth*, it pines, and faints to meet with the saints in the Lord's house. The desire was deep and insatiable—the very soul of the man was yearning for his God."[10]

God is going to give us many abilities in heaven. He will give us a resurrected body. He will give Himself to us in heaven. Let's start longing and preparing for that encounter now!

7

Heaven Is for Healing

Understanding the truths of heaven is what is healing our lives and has become our life message. These biblical realities have been our lifeline and our lifesaver. Over the next few pages, we'll examine some passages of Scripture to help you develop a heavenly perspective so that when you're going through earthly pain you will be able to make it. Candidly and from the heart, you need to know this: You can make it. You really can—through the grace of God and through the truth of His Word.

Randy Alcorn wrote in his book *Heaven*:

> The New Earth will be a place of healing. Christ's healing ministry was thus a foretaste of Heaven, the place where all hurts are healed, all suffering forever eclipsed by joy. Whenever Jesus healed people, the act spoke of wholeness and health, the original perfection of Adam and Eve, and the coming perfection of

resurrected bodies and spirits. Every healing was a memorial to the Eden that was and a signpost to the New Earth that will be.[1]

Why Do We Hurt?

Hurt and pain come from the fact that we live in a fallen world. Since Adam and Eve's massively bad decision making in the Garden of Eden, and the curse that was the result of their falling for Satan's lies, things have become crazy and hurt is all around us—and it seems, as we enter into what Jesus called the last days, it's increasing and getting worse.

Natural disasters happen because we live in a fallen world. The earth quakes and shakes—tornadoes, earthquakes, tsunamis, hurricanes, floods—because the earth is convulsing. It's living under the curse.

It is why wars happen. It's why strife and bigotry happen. Unredeemed, selfish, arrogant, and power-hungry people have a deep desire to wield ungodly authority over others. They are willing to go to war to get what they want. It's because of the curse. Their selfish appetites are no different from Eve's. She saw something she couldn't have and wanted it. She was willing to disobey God for what she wanted. Because of the fall and the curse, we live on a cursed earth, and consequently we have personal tragedies. Few things are perfect in our lives—we go through pain, sorrow, and hurt. We go through difficulties and tragedies because this is the world in which we live.

In their book *Does God Feel Your Pain?* H. Wayne House and William Grover further illustrate this critical thought:

> Suffering was not the original intention of God. He created a perfect world for Adam and Eve and their descendants—a world free from pain, whether physical, mental or spiritual. Unfortunately,

Adam and Eve gave in to temptation and fell from their perfect state, and sin entered God's perfect creation. The presence of sin in the world led to the presence of pain and suffering. . . . Today we suffer at the hands of this fallen world.[2]

It's interesting to read what the apostle Paul wrote concerning creation's response in this fallen world. Romans 8:22–23 says,

> We know that the whole creation groans and labors with birth pangs together until now. Not only that, but we also who have the firstfruits of the Spirit, even we ourselves groan within ourselves, eagerly waiting for the adoption, the redemption of our body.

God's creation, literally the whole earth, is convulsing and groaning. It's interesting that Paul uses the analogy of labor pains and birth. He's not simply using poetic or symbolic language—he's accurately describing what God is revealing to him. This whole earth is hurting, and so are we, the firstfruits (those who are born again and know God). We are groaning within ourselves—we are hurting and in pain because of sin that is part of this lost world.

Because of the fall and the curse, we live on a cursed earth, and consequently we have personal tragedies.

Paul, however, also points to hope. He says we are "eagerly waiting for the adoption." As believers in Jesus Christ, we are adopted into His family. This adoption will be fully realized when we get to heaven. While we may be groaning, we are also eagerly awaiting heaven.

Our adoption is critical to understand and hold in our hearts. Heaven is where our bodies will be redeemed. It is where everything is restored. When our hearts are firmly rooted in heaven, we can, with God's help, move through the pain and groaning because our perspectives are right. Our hearts can ache and our circumstances might not change, but we can have tremendous hope that in heaven we'll be redeemed and restored completely. Our heavenly perspectives can lead us to victory even in this fallen world.

We also need to understand that pain and sorrow happen to everyone. They happen to the just and the unjust alike. None of us are exempt because we live in this fallen world, and personal or natural catastrophes are going to happen.

Unfortunately, I've met too many Christians who are in trouble. They bought in to a toxic system of thinking that says, "If you have enough faith nothing bad will ever happen to you." Please don't buy in to that false ideology. We need look no further than Job. Scripture says, "[Job] was blameless and upright, and one who feared God and shunned evil" (Job 1:1). Here was a good man who faced tremendous pain and suffering. Daniel is another great example. He was a man of God who withstood treachery, several crazy kings, and being held in a lions' den. He was a man of great faith, yet he suffered pain and hardship.

Clearly pain and suffering can happen to anyone, anywhere.

We must understand that pain and suffering are results of the curse and the fallen world *before* something unwanted comes into our lives. We must understand this so that when something painful comes our way, we can understand why. We can point to the curse and know that it's nothing we've done—it's not because of a lack of faith. Understanding this also helps us know how we are going to get through it. When we know that pain is the result of this fallen world, our eyes won't be on the world looking for its way out—our eyes will look for a biblical perspective. In the midst of our pain and sorrow, we'll have a heavenly, not an earthly, mind-set.

Understanding the source and reality of pain and suffering is the difference between victory and defeat. It means when pain and sorrow come to your door, you won't answer it and say, "Oh my gosh, God, where are you? I've been faithful. I thought you loved me!" Preparation means having a heavenly mind-set and realizing this world is fractured and broken. While you don't welcome the pain, you stand on heaven's truth instead of human thought.

Heavenly Mind-Set

It's important for us to have a heavenly mind-set in the midst of our hurt so we can begin to be healed and fully experience the hope of heaven.

In Peter's Life

The apostle Peter is preaching in Acts 3:19–21. Pentecost has happened, and spiritually speaking, things are going very well. Right in the middle of his preaching Peter says,

> Repent therefore and be converted, that your sins may be blotted out, so that times of refreshing may come from the presence of the Lord, and that He may send Jesus Christ, who was preached to you before, whom heaven must receive until the times of restoration of all things, which God has spoken by the mouth of all His holy prophets since the world began.

Right after Pentecost Peter is talking about heaven. He is talking about Jesus being in heaven. He's talking about Jesus coming back from heaven and he's talking about what God said, through the prophets, about heaven and the issue of the restoration of all things. Peter, right from the start of his ministry, was heavenly minded.

109

What does Peter mean by the "restoration of all things"? It helps us to understand a bit more about this fallen world and God's desire for a time when the broken will be healed.

After the fall, God started speaking to the prophets about the time of the restoration of all things—when righteousness and justice would rule. Peter is reminding his audience that every one of the prophets pointed to this coming day, because God had told them, "You prophets, this fallen, cursed world isn't going to be the final word. I have something to do that is coming and I want you to start telling other people about it."

It's important for us to have a heavenly mind-set in the midst of our hurt so we can begin to be healed and fully experience the hope of heaven.

We can find the earliest account of this in Jude 1:14–15:

> Now Enoch, the seventh from Adam, prophesied about these men also, saying, "Behold, the Lord comes with ten thousands of His saints, to execute judgment on all, to convict all who are ungodly among them of all their ungodly deeds which they have committed in an ungodly way, and of all the harsh things which ungodly sinners have spoken against Him."

The seventh son from Adam talks about the return of the Lord with His saints to bring conviction to a sinful world. He's coming to right wrongs and to heal broken hearts.

The word translated *restoration* is used in wonderful ways. Jesus used it to speak of spiritual and moral things being restored. Josephus, the first-century Jewish historian, used the word *restoration* to speak of things that had been taken captive and would one day be restored. Philo of Alexandria, a philosopher who lived at the time of Jesus, used this same word to speak of financial things, the Year of Jubilee, and men being restored to their rightful inheritance. Physicians even used this exact same word to speak of health-related things—things that were wrong that would one day be restored and made whole.

When we put all of this together, it shows us something super important that we need to know about the heart of God in the midst of our hurt. From the beginning of time, God said there was a day coming when all hurting things, all broken things, and all things that are wrong would be restored. Spiritual and moral brokenness would be restored by heaven's holiness (2 Peter 3:13), captive and oppressed things would be restored by heaven's freedom (Luke 4:18), poor and impoverished things would be restored by heaven's riches and rewards (Matthew 5:12), and sick and hurting things would be restored by heaven's healing (Revelation 21:4).

Peter knew what was coming, and in his preaching he wanted the people to know how they could make it through the difficulties and hurt. He wanted them to develop a heavenly perspective, and he certainly had the personal experience and personal focus to prove his point.

God said there was a day coming when all hurting things, all broken things, and all things that are wrong would be restored.

Remember Peter, the apostle who denied Jesus three times but repented and was later restored by Jesus? That's the Peter who is speaking and who clearly understands restoration. He knows from personal experience Jesus' love and the importance of a heavenly mind-set while going through pain and suffering.

He witnessed it, he experienced it, and he is living it. Now he's telling this audience that they live in a cursed world, but God has a plan of hope, healing, and restoration, and if they commit themselves to having a heavenly mind-set, they'll make it through this troubled world victoriously.

In Paul's Life

Paul was faced with a troublesome dilemma. The Corinthian church was inundated with false teachers. These teachers (literally self-appointed apostles) were not only presenting an incorrect gospel, they were questioning Paul's apostleship. Part of the false teachers' new message included equating suffering and pain with weakness. In 2 Corinthians 4 Paul writes to show that weakness does not cripple people, but rather strengthens them. To Paul, weakness was not fatal; it was essential. Paul could write this because he lived it—he clung to a heavenly perspective and made it through the pain.

He writes in 2 Corinthians 4:8–10,

> We are hard-pressed on every side, yet not crushed; we are perplexed, but not in despair; persecuted, but not forsaken; struck down, but not destroyed—always carrying about in the body the dying of the Lord Jesus, that the life of Jesus also may be manifested in our body.

God brings life out of our toughest hurts. Paul says, "Sure, we feel the crush of pain. We don't always understand why we have pain and suffering, but we don't think we're hopeless or that God doesn't love us. Jesus' very life is in us during our suffering."

This is why Paul wrote later, "All things work together for good to those who love God, to those who are the called according to His purpose" (Romans 8:28). If you are hard-pressed, perplexed, in despair, persecuted, and struck down, God is going to bring life out of it and turn it around for your good if you'll hold on to Him and trust Him.

I know in the midst of your pain that verse from Romans can seem incredibly foreign to you. It can seem unreachable and unreal. Actually, you probably don't care because you are deeply hurting and wounded. You might not have any great prayers to pray and you are not filled with faith, excitement, and zeal for God. If you're in that place, let me tell you that I absolutely understand. You see, for the first several months of my grief, my private devotion with God consisted of three words: "Oh God, please!"

We hurt, and when we hurt sometimes the only thing we can say is, "Oh God, please!"

What Paul understood and what we must understand while we are in the depths of pain is that God gets it. He understands it. He responds to "Oh God, please!" When we have faith from a heavenly perspective in the midst of that kind of storm, He begins to turn it around and He begins to turn it into good. He begins to heal your heart and continues to heal your heart and makes you able to walk through it.

We may be struck down. We may feel hurt and sorrow, but we are not alone. When God comes through for us in the middle of unthinkable hurt, it foreshadows the ultimate download of goodness that we're all going to experience in heaven. Paul knew it and he lived it.

He writes, "Therefore we do not lose heart. Even though our outward man is perishing, yet the inward man is being renewed day by day" (2 Corinthians 4:16). Because God brings life and goodness out of hurt and pain, we don't lose heart. We don't quit, we don't give up, we don't walk away from Him, and we don't live hopelessly. We refuse to surrender to those things when our mind is focused on heaven.

How does that happen? Paul says, "We are renewed every day." Yesterday's renewing is insufficient for the hurt we feel today. I need to be renewed day by day. I need a fresh encounter with Jesus day by day—at times even minute by minute. Like Paul, some days you can look at my outside and see that I'm perishing. I'm falling apart. Inwardly, however, I'm spiritually renewed every day and every moment. The goodness, promises, and grace of God in heaven are upholding me.

Paul continues his encouragement to the Corinthians by saying, "For our light affliction, which is but for a moment, is working for us a far more exceeding and eternal weight of glory" (2 Corinthians 4:17).

Dr. Warren Wiersbe wrote,

> Note the contrasts Paul presented in 2 Corinthians 4:17: light affliction—weight of glory; momentary—eternal; working against us—working for us. Paul was writing with eternity's values in view. He was weighing the present trials against the future glory, and he discovered that his trials were actually working *for him*.[3]

Paul's "momentary light affliction" is mentioned more specifically in 2 Corinthians 11:24–28. He was lashed with a whip, beaten, and stoned; he was shipwrecked and met many perils; and he went without food, clothing, and heat. He had a life that was filled with suffering, but his heavenly mind-set allowed him to see afflictions as light and momentary. He realized that his afflictions were working in him a glory that surpassed anything we could imagine this side of heaven; his life wasn't for nothing. He saw that God was doing something even in the midst of the pain—He was conforming him into the image of Jesus and allowing him to enter into the fellowship of His sufferings. His pain was actually working for him.

I love what Paul wrote in Romans 8:18: "I consider that the

sufferings of this present time are not worthy to be compared with the glory which shall be revealed in us."

Paul is reassuring us that God's glory will far surpass our present circumstances. I know our pain is real, but when we start looking at pain through a heavenly lens and a scriptural, heavenly mind-set, suddenly we start considering all that God is preparing for us and we realize that there is no comparison between our present suffering and our future glory.

The phone rang—bad news. The test came back—bad news. Fill in the blank—bad news. Do you feel like your world is crumbling? Listen, I'm telling you from personal experience: When we look at things the way He has instructed us to look at things, through His heavenly lens, we will have hope and the healing process will begin. We will continue to wake up. We will continue to breathe. We will continue to put one foot in front of the next. We're not going to let up or slow down.

When we don't have a heavenly perspective, we shut down, we let up, and we quit. Our heavenly mind-set in the midst of our hurt makes all the difference in the world. If you are not there, I encourage you to read Paul's thoughts again. I encourage you to say, "Oh God, please!" Let Him, the God who loves you unconditionally, help you put on His heavenly perspective.

Second Corinthians 4:18 is one of those "therefore" moments. Paul is writing about pain and suffering, and then he wraps it up by saying, "We do not look at the things which are seen, but at the things which are not seen. For the things which are seen are temporary, but the things which are not seen are eternal."

> *Our heavenly mind-set in the midst of our hurt makes all the difference in the world.*

Paul is not going to focus on the *seen* hurts; he is not going to focus on the pain and the affliction that he goes through. He is going to focus on the *unseen*. He is going to focus on heaven and on eternity. He is going to focus on the promises of God and the coming restoration of all things.

Going back to the book of Romans, Paul wrote, "We were saved in this hope, but hope that is seen is not hope; for why does one still hope for what he sees? But if we hope for what we do not see, we eagerly wait for it with perseverance" (8:24–25).

Paul is writing about having a hopeful mind-set about heaven. He's saying that we are to wait for heaven's restoration, of all things, with eagerness and perseverance. We need to keep our eyes on the coming prize, not our current pain, and then healing and hope will happen.

Like Peter, Paul experienced it and then he wrote and spoke about it. He knew pain, but more important, he knew the hope of heaven and its ability to overcome pain and mend broken hearts.

In My Life

The example shown by these men's lives set the example of how to be heavenly minded, which enabled Sarah and me to live it out.

As a dad, I was looking forward to sharing certain milestones in Josiah's life: college, marriage, children. I dreamed of standing proudly by as he received his diploma from the University of Tennessee. I wanted to officiate at my son's wedding to his bride. And I definitely longed to hold Josiah's children—children that would have been our grandchildren. I remember puzzling over these thoughts, agonizing over them.

Early one morning, still turning these issues over and around in my mind, I finally poured out my complaint before the Lord just as David did (Psalm 142:2). I did all this in the shower. The shower is a fabulous place to get real. In the shower, I could sob and heave and cry out, unconcerned about being heard. In the shower, my tears and the water could run together. In the shower, I could come undone. And believe me, I did.

"What about college? What about marriage? What about children? What about all the things he will never, ever experience this side of heaven? What about those things, Lord?" I sobbed out questions that were some of the most emotionally charged I have ever asked aloud in my whole life. And there, in my bathroom shower, hidden away from everyone else but God, I finally heard the Lord speak.

"I have more than made up for these things."

I was stunned to silence. All I heard was the sound of water. After a minute, I spoke again.

"You mean more than marrying the love of his life, Lord? More than having kids?"

"Yes" came the kind answer. "I have more than made up for these things, Steve."

I understood in that moment what God was saying to me: Josiah was experiencing things so inexpressible—right at that very moment—that earth's best experiences could only pale in comparison. The Father's words to my heart began to settle the storm inside. At the very least, His promise put the shoreline back in my sight. And looking back, I see now that His words launched me on a journey toward the mysteries of heaven. It was one of those God moments that allow you to place a stake in the ground, where the revealed Word and a heavenly perspective change you in ways that are difficult to fully articulate.

> *Josiah was experiencing things so inexpressible— right at that very moment—that earth's best experiences could only pale in comparison.*

Please don't misunderstand me, the hurting still remains after my shower encounter, but God's answer to my pained complaint began the process of binding up a father's broken heart and bringing fresh hope to our family.

Know the Truth About Hurting

Hebrews 12:2 says, "Looking unto Jesus, the author and finisher of our faith, who for the joy that was set before Him endured the cross, despising the shame, and has sat down at the right hand of the throne of God."

Here are some important truths we need to put deeply into our hearts—whether we're hurting today or at a later time.

Look to Jesus in Your Hurt

Jesus knows your pain and hurt. He came to heal the broken and the brokenhearted. Too many people look at their hurt and they ignore Jesus, who is the author and finisher of our faith.

Know the Joy That Is Before You

Jesus knew restoration was coming. His mind was on heaven and the joy of all that heaven is and will be eternally. He knew the joy, and we need to know the same joy by maintaining a heavenly perspective.

Endure Your Cross

Because of the joy that is before you, and because of God's restoration of all things, you can make it through.

Despise the Shame

Jesus devalued the shame, the embarrassment, and the pain of being publicly crucified, and of everything else that He was going through. It means He didn't make a big deal about it. He chose to focus on heaven.

Sit in the Place of Power at God's Right Hand

When we apply these truths to our lives, we'll have a reserved seat at God's right hand (Ephesians 1:20; 2:6). When we overcome our hurt with God's healing and hope, by having a heavenly mind-set, we can take that next breath and that next step. We'll be able to face our today because we're looking at tomorrow.

Heaven Is Open

Mark 7:32–35 tells us,

> They brought to Him one who was deaf and had an impediment in his speech, and they begged Him to put His hand on him. And He took him aside from the multitude, and put His fingers in his ears, and He spat and touched his tongue. Then, looking up to heaven, He sighed, and said to him, *"Ephphatha,"* that is, "Be opened."

Jesus is touched by our weakness and pain. He weeps over the condition of this cursed world. He isn't sitting on the sideline heaving condemnation on us from a distance. He cares, He notices, and He bears our burdens with us.

Jesus, in the middle of His groaning sigh, looked to heaven. He's heavenly minded. Are you, in the midst of your groaning, looking to heaven?

119

Then Jesus asks for heaven to be opened. He's asking for heaven's power and glory to be opened to this man. Yes, He's asking for his ears to be opened, but Jesus takes it a step further. He wants heaven opened for this man. He wants heaven opened for you as well.

In your hurt, in your struggle and pain, ask Jesus to open heaven for you. He might do something instantly as He did for this fellow, or He could simply enlarge your heavenly perspective and give you new joy and revelation in what's coming. I can't predict what He will do, but I can say, from my own experience, that He will do something incredible. In opening heaven He will give you healing and eternal perspective. He will help you know that His grace is sufficient for you and the "light afflictions" you may be encountering. In the power of the Holy Spirit you need to say, "Heaven be opened. Show me the joy that is before me. I stand on your promises to restore and give me peace. Oh God, please."

8

Having Our Hands in the Harvest

Once we fully grasp all that heaven is and all that a heavenly focus gives us, we change. Our lives, attitudes, and priorities change the more our perspective changes from this world to the glory and majesty of heaven. Like Paul, we long to be with Jesus, but we also know we have a purpose for dwelling on earth.

As believers we are torn between two worlds. Our hearts are focused on the goodness and wonder of heaven, yet at the same time we more readily see the needs of people—we want to extend our hands to help them know the Savior through our testimony, our lives, and our service.

Our hearts are in heaven because of heaven's Savior—Jesus—and because of heaven's salvation—what He has done and how He has rescued our lives and forgiven our sins.

Our hearts are in heaven because of heaven's splendor, and everything that it *is* and everything that it *isn't*.

121

In this chapter, we are switching gears from looking at heaven to looking at what it means to have our hands in the harvest. Our hands are in the harvest because of heaven's sending. Jesus said to Paul, "Go. I want you to go" (see Acts 9:6). Paul immediately obeyed and started sharing Jesus in the synagogue (Acts 9:20). Throughout his ministry, Paul went where God led him to preach the good news of Jesus because of heaven's call (sending) upon his life.

Without question, we are to imitate the lifestyle of having our hearts in heaven and our hands in the harvest. It's not just for preachers. It's not just for apostles or prophets. It is for every believer. Paul said, "Imitate me, just as I also imitate Christ" (1 Corinthians 11:1). It's a mind-set we need to cultivate and live as long as we're here on this earth.

It's our mission to serve Jesus and serve others.

It's our mission to serve Jesus and serve others. John Stott wrote, "The Living God of the Bible is a sending God. . . . [He is] a missionary God!"[1] God accomplishes His mission through His followers. "The mission of God does not exist because of the church; the church exists because of the mission of God."[2]

We exist to fulfill God's mission. What is His mission? It's winning the lost, discipling the found, and sending the willing. God has called every one of us to live a lifestyle that is aligned perfectly with His mission.

The Shortage of Labor

There is a disconnect. We clearly see heaven's calling. We can clearly see Paul's encouragement, but we're not seeing an overabundance of workers in the harvest. Why?

Let's first look at a couple of curious Scriptures. The first one is Matthew 9:37–38, where Jesus says to His disciples, "The harvest truly is plentiful, but the laborers are few. Therefore pray the Lord of the harvest to send out laborers into His harvest."

The second one is Luke 10:1–2:

> After these things the Lord appointed seventy others also, and sent them two by two before His face into every city and place where He Himself was about to go. Then He said to them, "The harvest truly is great, but the laborers are few; therefore pray the Lord of the harvest to send out laborers into His harvest."

In both Scriptures Jesus makes it clear that the harvest (people who need Him) is plentiful. There are multiple opportunities for the gospel to go out and for people to be saved. There's incredible opportunity for the gospel to affect people's lives, for people to come to Christ, for people to be discipled in Christ, and for people to be sent out in Christ. He says, "It's white for harvest." That means the harvest is budding, it's ripe, it's ready to happen, and it's nonnegotiable for us to be involved with it.

The more curious part of this verse is that Jesus says, "But the laborers are few." According to Strong's Concordance, the Greek word used for *few* means "puny." The amount of laborers is not simply a small number; it's puny.

There's not a harvest problem. There are plenty of people who need the hope of heaven. There is a labor problem. There is a shortage of people who are willing to put their hands in the harvest.

It's interesting that the Creator of the universe would complain about a shortage of help. After all, He can do anything He wants, right? He can heal the sick and make the blind see.

He can raise the dead. If He can do all of that, why can't He do something to cure this labor problem?

Here's what we have to remember: If Jesus did it apart from our willingness, we'd miss the whole point. Our mission, as we described it just a few lines ago, is to have a heavenly perspective and serve the Lord in sincerity of heart. He doesn't force us; we serve Him because our hearts are first deeply rooted in Him and heaven.

Within those of us who have experienced God's love and salvation, far too often there's a disconnect between what we've received from God and what we actually do with what we've received. We see heaven, but we don't see the ripe and ready-to-be-gathered harvest. We experience God's love, but we don't show it to other people.

This disconnect leads to a shortage of laborers.

So why is there a shortage?

Over the next several pages I want to show you seven reasons for this shortage. Let me be clear, this is not meant to condemn or guilt people into trying to do something on their own for God. That's not my point; working in our own strength out of guilt isn't fulfilling God's mission. He wants our hearts, not our guilt-ridden, going-through-the-motions to-do list. Many of us simply need to make some adjustments. We need to examine our lives in light of what Scripture says and let it define who we are and help us change—repent, receive forgiveness, and start laboring.

Lack of Vision

Immediately before Jesus spoke about the plentiful harvest and few laborers in Matthew 9:37–38, it says in verse 36, "When He saw the multitudes, He was moved with compassion for them, because they were weary and scattered, like sheep having no shepherd."

I firmly believe that there is a shortage of laborers because we're not seeing the real spiritual condition of the multitudes. Jesus saw the multitudes and their condition. He saw their weariness. That word in the original language means "faint, despondent." One of the word's synonyms means "out of breath and fatigued."

Why were they weary and out of breath? From harassment, from harsh words, and from a spiritual void in their lives. Rome persecuted them and treated them harshly. They worked incredibly hard just to get by in life, and they had nothing to turn to except for a bunch of religious rules and regulations. They were harassed on all sides of their lives.

Jesus looked at the multitudes and saw weary, broken, and scattered people. He understood that the people were like sheep with no shepherd. They had no one to guide them, no one to provide for them, and no one to protect them.

Lack of Compassion

Jesus not only had a clear vision of them, but He also saw their condition and was moved with compassion. He saw opportunity, He realized there were not enough people with vision and compassion to help, and He responded to what He saw in front of Him.

What are you seeing in front of you today? When you notice need, are you moved with compassion to put your hand in the harvest? There are opportunities everywhere. The harvest is great. Every worker, no matter what they can do in the field, needs to be involved with the harvest. There's not a part of the harvest that's insignificant. But we first have to develop Christ's vision and compassion from our heavenly perspective.

Jesus said in John 4:35–36,

> Do you not say, "There are still four months and then comes the harvest"? Behold, I say to you, lift up your eyes and look at the fields, for they are already white for harvest! And he who reaps receives wages, and gathers fruit for eternal life, that both he who sows and he who reaps may rejoice together.

He's clearly telling us not to wait until someday in the future. He's saying that the harvest is right here in front of us, right now. We need to look up and know that with our hearts in heaven, we can make a difference no matter what we do in the harvest. Nothing is trivial and everything has with it an eternal reward.

Discomfort

Right before the passages in Luke 10:1–2, we read about an interesting encounter. Luke 9:57 says, "It happened as they journeyed on the road, that someone said to Him, 'Lord, I will follow You wherever You go.'"

He's saying that the harvest is right here in front of us, right now.

Jesus responded to this person in Luke 9:58–62. He basically told him that he didn't fully understand what he was signing up for. Jesus said that He didn't even have a place to lay His own head and it was going to be rather inconvenient and uncomfortable for anyone to follow Him. Laboring for Jesus Christ involves discomfort.

It's interesting to note that this person didn't respond. On one hand, he was ready to follow Jesus anywhere, but when he heard the reality of what that meant, he didn't even respond.

Working in the harvest is called *labor* for a reason. It's not called *ease*. There is a part of our Kingdom service that is often inconvenient and uncomfortable. New Testament professor Darrell Bock wrote,

> Jesus' directness and the shocking quality of his remarks here show just how seriously he takes the call to discipleship. The path to following Jesus is not a part-time job; it is a perpetual assignment. Since discipleship involves responding to people as well as to God, there is no moment when we are not "on call."[3]

Here's a key: We will be challenged by opportunities that are difficult and uncomfortable. Helping other people is not a nine-to-five job. Opportunities can't always be scheduled.

Rick Cua and Ron Gonzer are our church's pastors in charge of caring for people. Their care, concern, and love for others amazes me. It doesn't matter what time it is or what they are doing. They are available to care for hurting people. They lovingly meet and pray with people, coming alongside them for whatever they need. They are wonderful examples of men whose hearts are in heaven and because of that, their hands are deeply in the harvest, helping and loving people who need Jesus.

The harvest is plentiful. Are you letting your own feelings of discomfort get in the way of having your hands in the harvest?

Procrastination

Luke 9:59 says, "He said to another, 'Follow Me.' But he said, 'Lord; let me first go and bury my father.'"

This is one of those frequently misunderstood passages because of the way it's translated. At first we think that the man gave Jesus a good reason for not being involved in the harvest—he had to bury his father. But that's not what this verse means.

What the man was actually saying was, "*After* my father passes away, then I will come and follow you." He wasn't interested in following until sometime in the future after his father passed away and was buried.

This is what I call a "responsible excuse." In my nearly twenty-five years of pastoring I've seen many people not get involved in the harvest because of responsible excuses. They say something like, "I'll do it someday, as soon as _____." You can fill in the blank.

This man and others like him are simply putting it off. They are trying to cover up their procrastination with responsible excuses. They think, *I'll serve God later.*

> *Procrastination is a thief. It robs us of the opportunity to be involved in the major harvest that is right in front of us.*

Charles H. Spurgeon wrote, "We never shall have any time but time present . . . endeavor now to bring forth fruit."[4]

Friends, we don't have time for excuses and putting things off. Procrastination is a thief. It robs us of the opportunity to be involved in the major harvest that is right in front of us. We cannot let it steal the blessing of having our hand in the harvest and serving people who are weary, tired, and harassed. They need Jesus—now. Remember, many excuses are nothing but the skin of a reason stuffed with a lie.

Mistaken Priorities

Look again at the man who wanted to go home and bury his father. Jesus said to him, "Let the dead bury their own dead, but you go and preach the kingdom of God" (Luke 9:60). The first part seems rather harsh and insensitive. He was telling the man, "Let the spiritually dead deal with the issues of the physically dead." The spiritually dead are people who don't follow Him. Jesus realized the man was using his father as a responsible excuse. He took a moment and reaffirmed the cost of following Him.

He then told the man to preach the gospel. The man had his priorities mixed up, so Jesus emphatically told him the priority and demands of God's Kingdom.

How many of us have mistaken priorities? Jesus is saying that this—preaching the gospel—is *the* priority. We need to get connected to what Jesus is saying. Christianity is not simply about coming into a building, sitting down, singing some songs, shaking some hands, and listening to a feel-good-about-yourself message. It goes way beyond that. We need to have our priorities right, answer the call, and meet others' needs, because there is a shortage of laborers and the harvest is ripe. People are waiting and there are not enough workers.

Let's not allow mistaken priorities to get in the way of being profitable servants of God. Let's not explain away our refusal to get involved. Let's find ways to love Jesus and serve people by meeting their needs.

Selfishness

In this section of Luke, two men approached Jesus. Both wanted to follow, but they both had other things to do. They had responsible excuses and mistaken priorities.

It's interesting to me that both of these men used two words two thousand years ago that are spot-on for today's culture. They both used "me first." One said, "Let me first go and bury my father," and the other said, "Let me first say good-bye to those at my home" (Luke 9:61 AMP). They both had a "me-first" attitude.

The selfish me-first attitude has killed many a potential harvest laborer. We may know we're supposed to be involved in the harvest, but a me-first attitude prevents us from going very far because we're only interested in being served, not serving. Instead of realizing that the Kingdom of God is "others first," we want somebody to take care of us. Me first!

In 1906 Italian economist Vilfredo Pareto created a mathematical formula to describe the unequal distribution of wealth in his country, observing that 20 percent of the people owned 80 percent of the wealth. Interestingly, after Pareto made his observation, many others observed that it worked the same in other areas.

There has to be a change. Our me-first attitude needs to go.

The Pareto Principle, unfortunately, is alive and well in most American churches—20 percent of the people do 80 percent of the work and give 80 percent of the money. I refuse to give in to this principle! I refuse to say, "Well, if that's the principle, then that's how it needs to be with the church."

Our sights need to be set higher than this principle. We should aim to have 100 percent of the people do 100 percent of the work. The last thing in our lives should be an attitude that says, "Me first. I'm too busy. Let other people do it. I've got other things to do than serve."

There has to be a change. Our me-first attitude needs to go. Jesus is pointing to opportunities, and we cannot let ourselves get in the way of serving, reaching, and discipling people who need to know Him.

Fear

Fear is a huge reason that there is a shortage of laborers. Luke 9:61–62 says, "Another also said, 'Lord, I will follow You, but let me first go and bid them farewell who are at my house.' But Jesus said to him, 'No one, having put his hand to the plow, and looking back, is fit for the kingdom of God.'"

While this sounds like a reasonable request, Jesus called him out. Jesus told the man his motive wasn't about saying good-bye. It was about taking a step back before he even took a single step forward. The man was so paralyzed by fear that he couldn't step out and step up. He was only thinking about retreating.

Fear is subtle. It works hard to destroy even our best efforts. Here's how it works: There is a stirring in your heart. You see the harvest and you want to get involved. Then, even before "I'm going to do this" comes out of your mouth, fear creeps in and you start retreating. You say things like, "I can't do it. I don't know enough. I'll probably get it wrong. I haven't been a Christian long enough. I'm not a good enough Christian. I don't know enough people. So hey, Jesus, I'm going to get to that, but let me go with one of my responsible excuses and just say good-bye to my family."

The apostle Paul gave us encouragement to overcome our fears. In his letter to Timothy, his young, inexperienced protégé, he wrote,

> For God did not give us a spirit of timidity (of cowardice, of craven and cringing and fawning fear), but [He has given us a spirit] of power and of love and of calm and well-balanced mind and discipline and self-control.
>
> 2 Timothy 1:7 AMP

Paul was encouraging this young pastor who was facing a difficult time with his congregation. It was time for him to stand up and not be afraid. It was time for him to be fully engaged in the harvest with his congregation and use his God-given strengths to confront people who wanted to preach a false gospel and take over his leadership role. Paul told him to not let his fear short-circuit God's power.

Jesus cut to the chase. He said, "Nobody who puts his hand on the plow and looks back is even worthy of the Kingdom of God."

Fear. It keeps us from seeing and working in the harvest. It convinces us that we can't do it. Fear points us to responsible excuses, and we retreat. Beloved, we can do better than that.

The Solution

When there is a lack of vision and compassion, change is required. When we shy away because of discomfort, when we seek to procrastinate, and when we settle for misaligned priorities, change is required. When we're selfish or fearful, change is required. If our hearts are truly focused on heaven, we must make sure that our hands are in the harvest.

> Fear. It keeps us from seeing and working in the harvest. It convinces us that we can't do it.

How? There are some things we can do right now that will move us past these blocks to seeing and participating in the harvest.

Renew

The first step is to renew our heavenly perspective. We need to look inside ourselves in prayer, through God's revealing Word, and with help from the Holy Spirit to make sure our hearts deeply long for heaven. Typically when we allow these things to keep our hands from being fully engaged in the harvest, our hearts are not fully engaged with a heavenly vision and purpose.

Repent

Once our hearts are rooted firmly in heaven, we need to turn away from behavior that takes our focus from the great harvest.

Repentance turns us around from our excuses. As David did in so many psalms, we need to cry out to God and let Him bring change.

Receive Forgiveness

We need to ask God for forgiveness and a fresh attitude, and then we need to receive His forgiveness. God's forgiveness must be actively received. It's offered freely, but it is not truly experienced in our lives without a conscious, deliberate act of acceptance. When we confess to ourselves and to God that we are in need of forgiveness and turn to Him and receive it, He grants it freely and unconditionally.

Pray

We must seek God's will for our lives, and let Him show us both *where* to put our hands in the harvest and *how* to do it (let Him enable and empower us).

Obey

We cannot let distractions, attitudes, or excuses get in the way of serving. We need to obey God, move out, and develop an others-first eye that seeks to help and serve other people.

Truly having our hands in the harvest isn't about *if* we will serve. It is about *where* we will serve. When we renew our heavenly perspective, repent, and ask God to forgive us, we can be part of the solution and not part of the shortage of laborers.

Musician, pastor, and author David McGee wrote,

> God wants to do awesome things. People who forsake their own needs and wants by serving others demonstrate their focus is

on Jesus. The kind of humility that it takes to deny yourself to serve others is unnatural to humans, but through the incredible work of God it is made possible. There are more opportunities to serve others than there are of being served. Have you positioned yourself to serve or to be served?[5]

Ask God right now where you can serve. Ask Him for heavenly eyes that clearly see the harvest and how you can be involved in helping people and changing lives.

9

The Power of Knowing God's Word

Strong of Heart

It's important that we understand that we cannot do any harvest work without God's strength. We can't just go out and do something in our own strength. We must and should confess as the psalmist did, "O Lord, my strength" (18:1). God alone needs to be our strength.

God's strength comes to us through His Word and by His Spirit.

Several times in earlier chapters we've looked at the lives of Paul, Peter, and Jesus. Their ability to do what they did, even in the face of horrific and painful deaths, came from God's strength. They quoted His Word and they relied fully on His Spirit, not their own strength.

In the next two chapters we are going to dig deeply into His Word and His Spirit—two pillars that support our heavenly vision and opportunity to serve in the harvest. Each one brings us God's strength in different ways and at different times. Each one is critical to us to strengthen our hearts and help us when we start feeling weak in the knees.

Helping the Lost

There is a powerful moment in Acts 8:26–40. An angel of the Lord called Philip (not to be confused with the apostle Philip; this Philip was an early church deacon first introduced in Acts 6[1]) to take the road from Jerusalem to Gaza. On the way Philip met an Ethiopian man who served as treasurer for Queen Cadance—a very important man. The man was reading Scripture and ended up asking Philip for help. Acts 8:30 tells us,

> So Philip ran to him, and heard him reading the prophet Isaiah, and said, "Do you understand what you are reading?" And he said, "How can I, unless someone guides me?" And he asked Philip to come up and sit with him.

When we're going to serve with our hands in the harvest, we need to be equipped—we need the Word in us and we need to be in the Word.

Philip explained the Isaiah 53 passage the man was reading and told him "the good news about Jesus."

As they continued to travel, the Ethiopian saw water and asked Philip to baptize him.

Philip's obedience and quickness to respond give us an incredible example of having our hearts in heaven and having our hands in the harvest. He didn't question, he didn't wait, and he didn't find excuses. He ran toward the opportunity he saw and quickly embraced it.

This passage also shows us that Philip was prepared. When the Ethiopian man asked him for help, Philip didn't hesitate.

He didn't think, *I'm not going to put my hand in the harvest because I won't know what to say.* He had learned what to say.

This chapter looks into the importance of knowing God's Word. Because he knew God's Word, Philip was equipped to help the Ethiopian immediately. There were no excuses, and there was no waiting. When we're going to serve with our hands in the harvest, we need to be equipped—we need the Word in us and we need to be in the Word. When we are equipped, we can make a huge difference in other people's lives.

Disturbing Thoughts

Let me share with you some research that is extremely troubling.

- George Gallup, from the Gallup Polls, "has dubbed us 'a nation of biblical illiterates.' Only half of U.S. adults know the title of even one Gospel. Most can't name the Bible's first book."[2]

- "Americans love their Bibles. So much so that they keep them in pristine, unopened condition. Or, as George Gallup Jr. and Jim Castelli said in a widely quoted survey finding, 'Americans revere the Bible but, by and large, they don't read it.'"[3]

- Occasional Bible readers declined from 73 percent of Americans in the 1980s to 59 percent according to a recent Gallup Poll. Only 16 percent said they read the Bible daily.[4]

- "By the time most Americans reach the age of 13 or 14, they think they pretty much know everything of value the Bible has to teach and they are no longer interested in learning more scriptural content."[5]

- A survey sponsored by the Bible Literacy Project "yielded other distressing news. Only 34 percent of teens know what happened on the road to Damascus—where the Apostle

Paul was stunned into conversion by the appearance of God. Twenty-eight percent didn't know who Moses was."[6]

- "A 2005 study by the Barna Group asked American Christians to rate their spiritual maturity based on activities such as worship, service, and evangelism. Christians offered the harshest evaluation of their Bible knowledge, with 25 percent calling themselves not too mature or not at all mature."[7]

Something is really wrong with this picture. Professing Christians don't understand, nor do they read, their Bibles. The incredible opportunity they have to know God, His ways, and His will is lost. Scripture leads us to a personal encounter with Jesus Christ, and if it doesn't, we're missing the point completely. He *is* the Word.

When we're not actively reading and studying the Bible, the opportunity to use the Bible to help people know Jesus (as Philip did with the Ethiopian) is also lost.

We must be prepared and ready to reach out to people in need. Becoming intimately acquainted with God's Word is mandatory. It will prepare us for those times when we need to help someone.

The Attack of Opposition

If knowing the Bible is so important, why are so many people unfamiliar with it? Why do so many other priorities get in the way of the best way to know God, His will, and His ways?

In Mark 4:14–20 Jesus explains the parable of the sower. He gives us truth and clearly shows us why so many people are not reading and studying the Bible. He says:

The sower sows the word. And these are the ones by the way-side where the word is sown. When they hear, Satan comes immediately and takes away the word that was sown in their hearts. These likewise are the ones sown on stony ground who, when they hear the word, immediately receive it with gladness; and they have no root in themselves, and so endure only for a time. Afterward, when tribulation or persecution arises for the word's sake, immediately they stumble. Now these are the ones sown among thorns; they are the ones who hear the word, and the cares of this world, the deceitfulness of riches, and the desires for other things entering in choke the word, and it becomes unfruitful. But these are the ones sown on good ground, those who hear the word, accept it, and bear fruit: some thirtyfold, some sixty, and some a hundred.

First, notice that only 25 percent, or one out of four, of the soils produced fruit. Seventy-five percent, or three out of four, of the soils didn't produce anything. The people—represented by the soils in the parable—all heard the same message and had the same Word available to them, but only 25 percent actually did anything lasting with the truth they heard. We need to be among those who commit to read and study God's Word and let it produce fruit in our lives.

> *If knowing the Bible is so important, why are so many people unfamiliar with it?*

Second, I want to point out that serious spiritual opposition keeps us from hearing God's Word and doing God's Word. With the first soil, Jesus tells of how Satan comes immediately to steal the Word.

Satan is doing his best to steal God's Word from us. He engages in that spiritual conflict because he knows that if we receive and keep God's Word in our hearts, we will bear fruit. He cannot stand that idea. He "comes immediately and takes away the word" (v. 15).

Why aren't more people reading their Bibles and letting God's Word affect their hearts and actions? They give up when this opposition comes. Satan shows up, and they allow him to steal the Word from them.

We can't allow Satan to steal the Word from us, and Jesus gives us the reason: We will have no root in ourselves. We won't develop strong, Bible-based Christian character or commitment. When difficult times come, we won't have God's Word so deeply rooted in our hearts that we persevere. We miss the opportunity to grow through our trials. We miss the chance to be an example to others who are hurting and needing an encouraging word from someone who has been there and made it through victoriously.

Third, we see the Word choked out. Jesus said, "They are the ones who hear the word, and the cares of this world, the deceitfulness of riches, and the desires for other things entering in choke the word, and it becomes unfruitful" (vv. 18–19). Some people hear the Word, but they let their desire for riches and other things get in the way, and the Word is choked out of their lives. Their lust for natural, carnal, worldly things chokes out God's Spirit and the life of the Word of God. They allow the opposition of riches and desires to hold them captive to the world, instead of being captive to the Word. As we discussed in the last chapter, they develop a "me-first" attitude and let selfishness or misguided priorities paralyze them.

There is serious opposition against those of us who want to read and study God's Word.

There is serious opposition against those of us who want to read and study God's Word. We face satanic and worldly pressure to put our attention on everything but God's Word. If we want our hearts to know all that heaven has for us and to respond to God's calling to be in the harvest, we must stand up and make a commitment to read and study and do God's Word.

The Attack of Deception

We don't just face opposition to our reading of the Bible but also the attack of deception. Paul wrote to the young pastor Timothy, "Evil men and impostors will grow worse and worse, deceiving and being deceived" (2 Timothy 3:13). He echoes Jesus' message in Matthew 24, when He tells His disciples, "Don't be deceived" (vv. 4–5, 11, 24).

The Greek word for *deception* means "to seduce people into rebellion from the truth."[8] At the time Paul was writing to Timothy, there were people who were preaching a different gospel. They were trying to turn people's heads away from the pure message of Jesus and to a mixture of magic, Greek and Roman mythology, and some Christianity. Paul warned Timothy earlier in his first letter, "The Spirit expressly says that in latter times some will depart from the faith, giving heed to deceiving spirits and doctrines of demons" (1 Timothy 4:1).

The same thing happens today. If the devil can't keep God's Word from piercing your heart through his opposition, he will start twisting and perverting it. That's his attack of deception.

We saw deception at work in the Garden of Eden. The devil, the serpent, twisted and perverted what God said, and Eve fell for it. He tripped her up in his perversion of God's Word.

We have to understand Satan's opposition and deception. We have to know that he'll do anything to keep our Bibles from being read and obeyed. He'll do anything to keep them dusty old relics that sit nicely on a table. He'll do anything to keep our focus away from heaven and the harvest of people who want answers, help, and a Savior.

God, on the other hand, wants His Book in our hearts. He wants us to be fruitful and involved in the harvest, equipped and prepared.

Paul gives us the solution to this deception. He boldly wrote in 2 Timothy 4:2–4,

> Preach the word! Be ready in season and out of season. Convince, rebuke, exhort, with all longsuffering and teaching. For the time will come when they will not endure sound doctrine, but according to their own desires, because they have itching ears, they will heap up for themselves teachers; and they will turn their ears away from the truth, and be turned aside to fables.

First, he says, "Preach the word." He's encouraging this young pastor to stay focused on one thing—God's Word. Don't read from magazines, don't preach people's opinions, and don't preach about your summer vacation. Preach the Word and don't compromise or make an apology for it. Take God's Word, preach it, and see how it changes people's lives.

Second, Paul tells Timothy to do it with conviction. If you need to rebuke people, do it. If you need to warn them, do it. If they need exhortation, do it. Take God's Word and preach it with conviction. Don't hold back and never stop preaching the Word.

Then Paul gives Timothy a warning. He tells him about a day that's coming when people (believers and nonbelievers) will not endure sound doctrine. People are going to turn away from God's truth and find teachers who will tell them what they want to hear and not care whether God has anything to do with it.

We see this happening today. People just want to hear what feels good to hear. They don't want to be challenged or convicted.

They don't want to hear about unselfish, sacrificial living or responsibility. They fall for deception. They fall into false teaching and fall away from God's Word.

A few verses earlier Paul wrote,

> You must continue in the things which you have learned and been assured of, knowing from whom you have learned them, and that from childhood you have known the Holy Scriptures, which are able to make you wise for salvation through faith which is in Christ Jesus.
>
> 2 Timothy 3:14–15

These verses jump from the page at me. Paul says, "You must continue." It's an admonition to Timothy to keep going, keep fighting, and keep pressing into God's Word. Paul's saying, "Don't concern yourself with arriving; you never will. But you can keep learning and reading, and you'll continue to discover new vistas to explore in God's Word."

Have you ever reached a place where you stopped continuing?

I want to ask you a question. Have you ever reached a place where you stopped *continuing*? Have you fallen into the opposition trap? Or the deception trap? Are you like the people Paul wrote about, saying, "Though by this time you ought to be teachers, you need someone to teach you again the first principles of the oracles of God; and you have come to need milk and not solid food" (Hebrews 5:12)? Have you stopped *continuing* and want only milk?

Don't be deceived. Warren Wiersbe wrote,

> The purpose of Bible study is not just to understand doctrines or be able to defend the faith, as important as these things are. The

143

ultimate purpose is the equipping of the believers who read it. It is the Word of God that equips God's people to do the work of God.[9]

We must continue to continue. We must make it a priority to know God's Word and have it deeply rooted in our hearts. We must be equipped so we can be prepared.

Unfortunately most of us just want to be saved from hell, but God wants us saved from hell so we can save others from hell. God wants us saved from fear and panic. God wants us to be ready to defend our faith, not out of ego or religious rigidness, but out of His love and kindness that we can only discover if we read His Word and get to know Him and the promises of heaven. We can't give away what we don't know.

We will not face one thing in our own lives or as we reach out into the harvest that isn't covered in the Bible. It has all the answers we need for those we're helping. We just need to dig them out, like golden nuggets.

Let's not be deceived. Let's continue to grow and learn from God's Word. Let's allow it to convict us and change us, and let's not back down from preaching it to people who need to hear it. Whether you call it preaching, witnessing, or sharing the gospel, it's a command for every believer, not just the paid clergy!

The Authority of Scripture

When our Enemy tries to deceive us or oppose us, he typically attacks the authority of Scripture, and we need to refuse to listen to his lies.

Paul wrote to Timothy,

All Scripture is given by inspiration of God, and is profitable for doctrine, for reproof, for correction, for instruction in righteousness, that the man of God may be complete, thoroughly equipped for every good work.

2 Timothy 3:16–17

All of Scripture, from Genesis to Revelation, is God-breathed. God inspired it. People did not invent it. Peter said the same thing in 2 Peter 1:21: "Prophecy never came by the will of man, but holy men of God spoke as they were moved by the Holy Spirit." The Spirit inspired men who wrote the Word. All of Scripture is *profitable*, which means "helpful, useful, and advantageous." The Word is profitable for learning, for truth, and for reproof (meaning conviction). The Word is profitable for correction (straightening us out) and for instruction in righteousness (guiding us in the right direction). The Word is profitable to make us complete and mature in the Lord. It can thoroughly equip us to live on this fallen earth and know how to reach out to people in the harvest.

I love what R. C. Sproul wrote about God's Word: "The Scriptures function as our chief reprover, our chief corrector and our chief trainer."[10]

It's not as much about where I've taken this Bible as it is where this Bible has taken me.

I love my Bible. My mom gave it to me on Christmas in 1984. I write down places I've taken it and it's taken me. It's been to Canada, the Dominican Republic, New Zealand, Israel, Italy, Mexico, England, Switzerland, Ghana, Germany, Ukraine, Uganda, Jordan, Iraq, Kenya, and Haiti. My Bible has been completely re-bound and re-covered. It goes everywhere with me.

But it's not as much about where I've taken this Bible as it is where this Bible has taken me. For over twenty-five years this Bible has brought the truth of God's Word into my life. Any decent thing that I am, or that I've become—dad, husband, son, preacher—is because of what I've read and obeyed in this Book. I've given it a chance. I've believed it, and I've seen that it's true. I do my best to continue to dig out the treasures that are in it and give my life for its cause.

The Bible. The Word of God. It fills you, blesses you, and gives you wisdom, understanding, knowledge, hope, and truth. It gives you power. It changes your life. It gives you something to share with other people all over the world who are desperate and in need. Stand on it. It has life-giving power.

The Power of Scripture

Scripture is full of power, and we need to take advantage of that power as we continue reading it, studying it, and using it to help others see Jesus through their hurt. For our purposes in this chapter, there are four areas of power in God's Word that I want to share.

Truth and Freedom

John 8:31–32 says, "Jesus said to those Jews who believed Him, 'If you abide in My word, you are My disciples indeed. And you shall know the truth, and the truth shall make you free.'"

Jesus calls us to abide in His Word. It means that we should focus and meditate on it. John Piper wrote, "This cannot mean merely, 'Keep my commandments.' Rather it means, 'Keep on trusting my word. Keep on trusting what I have revealed to you about myself and my Father and my work.'"[11] When we abide in His Word, we know the truth. Deception and opposition are defeated because we are immersed in the truth of God. We have the power to shut down the Enemy's negative voice.

146

Jesus also says that when we know the truth, we'll be free. Freedom comes from knowing God's truth about Himself and about yourself. Freedom comes from knowing who God is: His promises, character, and will. It also comes from knowing who you are in Christ. You can only learn those things by reading and studying the Bible.

The Bible powerfully and wonderfully gives you the truth that will set you free. Do you want to be free? Discover the truth of the Word.

Spirit and Life

Jesus says in John 6:63, "The words that I speak to you are spirit, and they are life." The Word is Spirit and it takes the Holy Spirit, who is the Spirit of Truth (John 16), to make the Word real and alive to us. It takes the Holy Spirit's enlightening to give us revelation and help us understand.

A natural person has difficulty understanding the Bible. But when we read it with a spiritual willingness to listen and obey, we'll understand it. We need to approach it with a heart that says, "Spirit of Truth, guide and lead me into all of God's Truth. Speak to me. Let me see Jesus' heart. I'm hungry to hear His voice. Show me." If we do that, the Holy Spirit will be quick to bring understanding to us.

We can't approach Jesus' Word as we approach a to-do list. As much as I appreciate one-year Bible reading programs, we cannot access the power of Scripture by reading a couple of chapters and then forgetting about them as we go out and do our own thing. The power of the Word is not going to pierce our hearts if we simply read it as natural people and don't let it marinate in our hearts and minds.

Sure, we can read the Bible from unilluminated, unspiritual

hearts, but it will do absolutely nothing for us. The religious Jews in Jesus' time studied like crazy. They memorized huge portions of Scripture. Yet Jesus said, "You search the Scriptures, for in them you think you have eternal life; and these are they which testify of Me. But you are not willing to come to Me that you may have life" (John 5:39–40).

> *The power of the Word is not going to pierce our hearts if we simply read it as natural people and don't let it marinate in our hearts and minds.*

He's showing them the difference. He's pointing to the power Scripture has to guide and lead us into truth. He's telling them that a Spirit-led encounter with His truth will lead them to a personal relationship with Him, not just a checked-off list of memorized verses.

The power of Scripture comes from asking God's Spirit to lead and direct our reading and study of His Word. That commitment leads to life—a deeply personal and satisfying relationship with Jesus Christ. Then it leads us to reach out into the harvest with boldness and confidence. It becomes our trusted partner as we talk with, work among, and minister to others.

Countless Benefits

Psalm 119 contains 176 verses, and the subject of the psalm is the glory of the Word of God. Here's my personal summary of Psalm 119 and the countless benefits of the power of Scripture.

If you give yourself to the Word of God you'll be blessed. You won't walk in iniquity (you won't deliberately sin), you will walk in God's ways, and you won't live a shameful life. Praise will erupt from your heart. You'll be cleansed, you won't wander aimlessly through life, and you won't give yourself to habitual sin. You will delight in meditating on God's Word, you won't be forgetful of the Word, and you'll see wondrous things in the Word because the Holy Spirit will illuminate your spiritual eyes. You will receive counsel, you will be revived, you'll be strengthened, and your heart will be enlarged in a good, healthy, spiritual sense. You will understand the Word; you will have salvation, trust, hope, consistency, liberty, life, and comfort. Songs will erupt in your heart from knowing and meditating on the Word of God. You will have clarity, vision, and steadfastness. You will receive mercy, wisdom, direction, single-mindedness, power over sin, and redemption. You will be awestruck by the Word of God. You will have peace, stability, and help.

R. A. Torrey wrote about the Bible,

There is power in this Book, when it is properly studied, to make and keep the life clean that no other book possesses. And there is also in this Book, when properly studied, a power that no other book possesses, to make and keep the heart pure.[12]

A Ready Defense

The power of Scripture gives us truth and freedom, Spirit and life, and bountiful blessings. It also gives us a defense against attacks.

First Peter 3:15 says, "Sanctify the Lord God in your hearts, and always be ready to give a defense to everyone who asks you a reason for the hope that is in you, with meekness and fear." The apostle is telling us to set God and His Word first in our lives and then be prepared to give people answers out of the hope that the Word has set in our hearts.

As a new, young Christian who drove a parts truck for a local Cadillac dealer in Southern California, I spent hours every day listening to Dr. Walter Martin, "The Bible Answer Man."

First Peter 3:15 was Dr. Martin's life verse, and he was always prepared to defend his faith and the Bible.

For hours every day, I would listen to people call in to the show with questions. I felt like I was in parts-truck seminary. It got to the point where someone would call in *and I knew the answer*!

There's no thrill like sitting with someone who has a question about God and with boldness, confidence, and the Spirit's anointing being prepared to answer it. There is nothing that can compare with giving someone His Word and watching it pierce his or her heart. It's such a privilege, yet it doesn't happen if we're not equipped with the Word.

> *There is nothing that can compare with giving someone His Word and watching it pierce his or her heart.*

Peter was ready. When the Spirit of God fell upon early church leaders at Pentecost, they were accused of being drunk. Peter, however, stepped up to the plate (Acts 2:14–40). He quoted Joel 2:28–32 and delivered a three-and-a-half-minute sermon that resulted in over three thousand people coming to Christ. Peter was ready to give an answer for the hope that was within him. He knew the power of Scripture and he used it to defend his faith and lead others to Jesus.

People are in need. People you meet, people who live next door, and people with whom you work. They need help, freedom, love, and hope. Are you prepared to give them God's Word? Is God's Word in your heart so you can reach out to the harvest? Or does it lie unopened, helping no one?

Recommitment to Scripture

Second Timothy 2:15 tells us, "Be diligent to present yourself approved to God, a worker who does not need to be ashamed, rightly dividing the word of truth." There isn't a shortcut to knowing and studying Scripture. You are not going to understand it unless you read it yourself. It doesn't come to us through osmosis. Yes, we can read other books or listen to solid Bible teachers, as I learned from Dr. Walter Martin, but nothing comes close to our own personal encounter with God's Word. Nothing comes close to hearing directly from God's Word and applying it to our individual lives and circumstances.

We have to study and we have to labor. We have to dig it out for ourselves. We have to find answers to our own questions through the Holy Spirit's guiding and leading. The phrase "rightly divide" implies a cutting through something or cutting straight, as in the exactness of a carpenter's precision. We are told to carefully cut through the Word so we can understand it and help other people understand it.

It's radically important that we show ourselves approved. It means we're looking for answers and willing to help other people find answers. It means we're continuing in our maturing and seeking God's Word to set us free from deception and opposition.

We're workers. There's a harvest of blessing and treasure in the Scriptures, but we have to dig them out. It takes labor to mine the riches of the Word. We have to work to discover what God wants us to hear and share. It takes time and effort to know the voice of deception and how to combat it.

God has given us the truth. We cannot let it slip away from us. We can't make excuses. There are people who need to hear His voice, and we are the ones who are called to reach into the harvest and give it to them.

We need to repent of neglecting Bible reading and letting His Word be stolen from us by the Enemy's deception and opposition. We need to repent from not having any roots in ourselves and consequently stopping our reading and study of the Word when things get tough, or worldliness comes and chokes it out. We need to repent from reading cerebrally and not spiritually. We need to repent from not studying diligently, and not having answers for seekers. We need to repent, receive forgiveness, and recommit to being people who study the Word and experience God, and then touch others with God's truth.

The harvest is plentiful and we have the very Word of God to encourage, help, and minister to people. We have every opportunity to read it, learn it, and let it support us in the work He has called us to do.

For guidance in your study of the Bible, please see the Bible Study Resources section at the end of the book.

10

The Power of the Holy Spirit

In the upper room, Jesus promised to send the Holy Spirit (John 14:16–18). Clearly we see from His conversation with the apostles that we cannot live the life God intended for His children apart from the help of the Holy Spirit.

If we are going to have our hearts rooted in heaven and our hands stretched out in the harvest in an effective way, we must know the Word and follow Jesus' commandment to be empowered by the Holy Spirit.

George Barna gives us another sobering statistic to consider. "The two aspects of spiritual life that people were most likely to acknowledge struggling with were 'sharing your faith with others' . . . and 'Bible knowledge.'"[1] This survey revealed that 76 percent consider themselves average or below average in sharing their faith.

The reason we are so unsuccessful in witnessing is often directly linked to our lack of spiritual power, power that Jesus promised (Acts 1:8) before He ascended.

God's Word, which we discussed in the last chapter, and the Holy Spirit are the two most important power sources for Christians. The Bible gives us power to know God, defend our faith, and reap countless benefits. The Holy Spirit gives us power to share our faith with other people and meet their needs. In the next few pages we're going to walk through the power of the Holy Spirit.

We'll look at the role of the Holy Spirit in the life of Jesus and the early church. Then we'll explore what it means to be "continually filled" with the Spirit, and how to be filled with the Spirit so you can have your hand in the harvest in an effective and powerful way.

The Role of the Holy Spirit in Jesus' Life

We see the Holy Spirit's presence in Jesus as He sought to put His hand in the harvest and change lives. Luke 4:18–19 says,

> The Spirit of the Lord is upon Me, because He has anointed Me to preach the gospel to the poor; He has sent Me to heal the brokenhearted, to proclaim liberty to the captives and recovery of sight to the blind, to set at liberty those who are oppressed; to proclaim the acceptable year of the Lord.

Jesus tells us directly that the Spirit of God is upon Him. He filled Him. The Holy Spirit came upon Him for a very specific reason—there was a gospel to share and there was (harvest) work to do.

Just as the Spirit of God filled Jesus, we need that same filling to come upon us with power. This filling is not so we can experience some kind of spiritual charge. Jesus said, "The Spirit of the Lord is upon me *because* . . ." That implies a purpose and a cause. There were people with needs. There were people to serve. There were people to save.

Jesus was also saying, "I have to do this work and it takes the Spirit's power and filling for Me to do it." Jesus the Man clearly recognized that He couldn't do it alone. He understood that He needed the filling of the Holy Spirit to do the work that was in front of Him. He recognized the harvest, He saw the needs, and He knew He could not do anything in His own human power. This is a powerful lesson for us.

In John 17:18 Jesus prayed to the Father. He said, "As You sent Me into the world, I also have sent them into the world." He sent out His disciples the same way the Father sent Him—anointed by the Spirit of God. How does the Son send out His church? The same way—anointed by the Spirit of God.

The Person and the power of the Holy Spirit must find His way into our lives. He gives us the power to overcome the fear that binds us from serving when we see other people's needs. He gives us the boldness to share our faith.

The Role of the Holy Spirit in the Early Church

Provided Patience and Power

We're going on a journey through the book of Acts and we're going to see how the Holy Spirit gave the apostles boldness. He came alongside of them and not only guided them but also gave them the power to do what God called them to do.

This is not simply a history lesson. I want you to see, right from Scripture, not just how the early church relied on the Holy Spirit to do what God called them to do, but also what your life might be like as a Christian if you completely yield to, fully receive, and totally obey the Holy Spirit.

Our journey starts in Acts 1:4–8.

First you need to realize that Jesus commanded the apostles to wait for the promise of the Father before they began doing His work. It wasn't a suggestion. Jesus gave the disciples the Great Commission (Matthew 28:16–20). Then He asked them to wait to receive the Holy Spirit—the power and presence of the Spirit was that important for them to have before they went out and put their hands in the harvest.

Jesus commanded the apostles to wait for the promise of the Father before they began doing His work.

The second thing you need to realize is that Jesus said He was going to give us the power to be witnesses. He didn't hesitate. He boldly proclaimed that we would be given power to witness for Him.

The word *power* comes from the Greek word *dunamis*. It's where we get our word *dynamite*. It signifies explosive power. The Holy Spirit gives us that kind of incredible TNT power so we can be witnesses of the person, work, and love of Jesus Christ to a world that's gone mad.

They were told to wait, and after days of praying and waiting the power came.

Filled People With the Spirit

Ten days after the apostles received this command from Jesus, "They were all filled with the Holy Spirit and began to speak with other tongues, as the Spirit gave them utterance" (Acts 2:4).

I don't want to debate whether speaking in tongues is relevant for today, or if it's real. That's not the issue for this chapter or this book. What is important to notice is when the Holy Spirit comes upon you, you start talking!

156

Acts 2:11 says, "Cretans and Arabs—we hear them speaking in our own tongues the wonderful works of God." The Holy Spirit empowered them and they began to declare how good and marvelous God is. Is there evidence in your life, based on what you boldly say about God, that you've been filled with the Holy Spirit?

Gave Boldness

In the last chapter we looked at Acts 2:14–40. We need to examine it again and see the Holy Spirit's role. Peter was preaching. He prophesied—literally speaking divinely inspired words. He spoke with the help and power of the Holy Spirit. He did not speak words that had a human origin; he spoke words directly from the Holy Spirit that caused over three thousand people to say, "I need Jesus Christ."

Peter, filled with the Holy Spirit, stood up. This is the defining characteristic of the work of the Holy Spirit. When the Holy Spirit touches your life with power, He will cause you to speak up and stand up. He will cause you to be stronger than you've ever been on your own.

Peter stood up and spoke up. The Holy Spirit gave him power, boldness, and conviction to be a witness for Jesus Christ. Often we think we have to speak up, but we shrink back because we look to our own limited abilities instead of fully relying on the Holy Spirit. The Spirit of the Lord came upon Peter and he stood up and spoke, not on his own strength, but in the strength of the Spirit.

Peter said, "Heed my words." Infused with the Holy Spirit, he stood up and boldly said, "Listen up! I have something important to tell you." He wasn't simply blathering words to bring attention to himself. He wasn't pandering to the crowd. He looked them in the eye and shared under the control and power of the Holy Spirit.

Peter brought clarity to the situation. He quoted from the book of the prophet Joel and brought simple yet profound teaching. He didn't have an Old Testament scroll from which to read. He didn't have the latest smartphone Bible app. He presented the Word of God, which was hidden in his heart. He quoted half a chapter of Joel, and the Word of God, sharper than any two-edged sword, pierced people's hearts.

In the last chapter we looked at the importance of knowing God's Word. Peter was a simple fisherman. We know he didn't have much education (Acts 4:13). He worked with his hands. He didn't go to Bible school, but he knew his Bible. He studied under Jesus' teaching and he relied on the Holy Spirit to help him share what he knew. It's the Word in us that the Spirit will enliven, embolden, and enflame when we need it in our harvest work.

In boldness Peter stood up, spoke, and brought the Word. Acts 2:37–38 shows us what happened:

> When they heard this, they were cut to the heart, and said to Peter and the rest of the apostles, "Men and brethren, what shall we do?" Then Peter said to them, "Repent, and let every one of you be baptized in the name of Jesus Christ for the remission of sins; and you shall receive the gift of the Holy Spirit."

What happens when we're bold enough to put our hand in the harvest, after being filled with the power of the Holy Spirit, and speak the Word? People's hearts are pierced. The Spirit-directed Word of God cuts open bruised and broken hearts, and brings conviction, understanding, and salvation. People who are lost find God.

Peter boldly told the people to repent. He didn't mince any words. He told them they needed to quit running away from God and start running toward Him. He told them about God's love and forgiveness, and that it was available to them if they would just repent (change direction). This doesn't merely mean to adjust our course. True repentance takes a turning away from sin. A slight change in direction won't do. It's completely turning to God with a 180-degree directional change.

Here's an interesting observation. Peter was simply telling others to do what he himself had done: believe, repent, be forgiven, and be filled with the Spirit. He essentially said, "God led me to repent, be forgiven, and receive the Holy Spirit, and He will do the exact same thing for you." He told them something they could not refute or argue against because it was his personal experience. People can argue about all kinds of things, but they cannot argue about *your* story. It's your changed

> *It's the Word in us that the Spirit will enliven, embolden, and enflame when we need it in our harvest work.*

life. People may argue or take issue with your testimony, but nothing changes the fact that yours is a life that was eternally changed by Jesus!

We should take a lesson from Peter and boldly share our story of how God saved us, how He forgave us, and how the Holy Spirit is daily renewing and making us more like Jesus.

We may not see the final result—sometimes we do and sometimes we don't. But God rewards our boldness and faithfulness. The end result is not our responsibility; it's the Holy Spirit's responsibility to take that convicted heart and begin to turn it. We can't do it on our own. We simply need to be like Peter and stand up and speak the Word to people who need to hear it.

We see Peter's boldness again in Acts 4:7–13. Peter and John were preaching and healing (see Acts 3). The religious people were uptight and started persecuting the church. They wanted answers and the situation became more volatile.

In Acts 4 Peter, filled with the Holy Spirit's power and boldness, was uncompromising. He looked at the Jewish leaders and said, "There is no other name given under heaven among men by which you can be saved—except the name of Jesus Christ" (v. 12, my paraphrase).

Peter laid his life on the line. He took a stand. What was the result? People marvelled at him and John. They saw strength in these men who stood for principles in which they deeply believed. The people saw conviction.

How did this happen to "uneducated and untrained men" (Acts 4:13)? They were fishermen who were filled with the Word and filled with the Spirit. They spoke the truth under the anointing of God, and the results were visible. The religious leaders, who were smart and studied all their lives, were amazed by what they witnessed.

Simply said, being filled with the Spirit and spending time in God's Word are two essential qualifications for having your hand in the harvest.

Continually Filling

There was a prayer meeting in Acts 4. The church was experiencing tremendous persecution and the disciples gathered to pray. They said,

"Lord, look on their threats, and grant to Your servants that with all boldness they may speak Your word, by stretching out Your hand to heal, and that signs and wonders may be done through the name of Your holy Servant Jesus." And when they had prayed, the place where they were assembled together was shaken; and they were all filled with the Holy Spirit, and they spoke the word of God with boldness.

Acts 4:29–31

Their prayer was to speak the Word boldly. Their prayer wasn't, "God, make our circumstances easier. God, make them quit being mean to us!" Quite the contrary. They asked for the ability to speak God's Word boldly. They made it clear that they were still committed to God's will and way even in the midst of harsh opposition.

God honored their prayer and filled them again! If you check out the back story, you'll see that they received the Holy Spirit in John 20, they received the Holy Spirit in Acts 2, and they received the Holy Spirit again in Acts 4. God filled them again and they went out and, indeed, they spoke the Word with boldness. Being continually filled with the Holy Spirit is exactly what the apostle Paul taught in Ephesians 5:18. He wrote, "Do not be drunk with wine, in which is dissipation; but be filled with the Spirit." The meaning in the original Greek is "but be continually filled; get filled over and over and over again."

Jesus didn't say, "You *might* receive power and boldness when the Spirit comes upon you"; He said, "You *shall*" (Acts 1:8, emphasis mine).

With all humility, I have to say that anyone who tells you that you have every bit of the Holy Spirit the moment you come to Jesus is not accurate. All you have to do is look in the Word at the apostles' lives. As I wrote earlier, there are three accounts of times when they were filled with the Spirit. The apostles are examples of what Paul said believers should do—they were continually filled.

161

Our mission to be part of this plentiful harvest depends on our continual filling of the Holy Spirit. As

> *Our mission to be part of this plentiful harvest depends on our continual filling of the Holy Spirit.*

we work to help others and as we share our faith in our neighborhoods and workplaces, we desperately need the ongoing filling of the Holy Spirit. We continually need the patience, power, and boldness of the Holy Spirit. This is how the Kingdom of God gets expanded. This is how we can have our hearts in heaven and our hands in the harvest, doing eternal work for God's glory.

As we read on in the book of Acts, we find more accounts of believers being filled with the Holy Spirit:

- The Samaritans receive the Word of God and are filled with the Spirit (Acts 8:14–17).
- Saul of Tarsus, or the apostle Paul, is filled with the Spirit (Acts 9:17).
- Cornelius, a Roman centurion, and other Gentiles in his house are filled with the Holy Spirit (Acts 10:44–46).
- The apostle Paul is filled again (Acts 13:9–10). He personally experiences what he later wrote about in Ephesians 5:18.
- Some unnamed disciples are filled with the Holy Spirit and joy (Acts 13:52).
- Ephesian believers are filled with the Holy Spirit (Acts 19:6).

We see the Holy Spirit continually filling believers so they can boldly proclaim God's Word and boldly do God's work and will. His filling is not something that just happens once—it should happen continually to refresh us in power and boldness.

Two Warnings

We can choose to try to do things on our own and not let the Holy Spirit work in and through us. We can choose to ignore the Holy Spirit or simply not ask for His help. As we start to put our hands in the harvest, we need to be careful. We need to remember how Peter approached the task, with biblical knowledge and spiritual power, and take two warnings from Paul seriously.

Grieving the Holy Spirit

Paul wrote in Ephesians 4:30, "Do not grieve the Holy Spirit of God, by whom you were sealed for the day of redemption." Grieving the Holy Spirit is doing what the Holy Spirit says *not* to do. *Grieving* literally means to "afflict with sorrow and sadness." Grieving the Holy Spirit is walking in disobedience—doing what God says not to do. When we grieve the Holy Spirit, we diminish His power to transform us.

There are many examples of this in the Old and New Testaments. The Holy Spirit came mightily upon Samson several times (Judges 13:25; 14:6, 19; 15:14), but left him as he persisted in sin. When King Saul was disobedient, the Holy Spirit departed from him (1 Samuel 16:14). Stephen rebuked the Jewish leaders (Acts 7:51) about their resistance to the Holy Spirit.

Grieving the Holy Spirit leaves us without the power to overcome the deception and destruction of the devil. We're left on our own to try to work things out and as I've shared, that's not the way Kingdom work is done. Be warned: Don't grieve the Holy Spirit. The only road to follow is one that leads to a closer walk with God and His Word and invites the Holy Spirit's leading and power.

Quenching the Holy Spirit

Paul wrote in 1 Thessalonians 5:19, "Do not quench the Spirit." *Quenching* was a firefighting term used to explain how to put out a fire. Paul is telling us that we dare not extinguish the Holy Spirit. We shouldn't silence Him when He's speaking to us. Quenching the Spirit is *not doing* what He says to do.

Here we have opposite ends of the same issue. On the one hand, when we grieve the Holy Spirit, we're doing what He says not to do. On the other hand, quenching the Spirit is not doing what He says to do. Paul tells us not to do either one because both grieving and quenching the Holy Spirit restrict His work in us and through us. We won't have any of His power or boldness because we're either doing what we shouldn't do or we're not doing what we should do. We're either making Him sad or we're throwing a wet blanket on Him.

Unfortunately, the average Christian doesn't realize the severity of grieving and quenching the Holy Spirit. We don't realize how much we restrict Him from flowing through our lives and anointing us with power to do Kingdom work. We don't understand how much we restrict Him when we walk in continued, unconfessed disobedience. We need to continually invite the Holy Spirit into our lives and hearts. Being filled with the Holy Spirit is not just a one-time event. It's ongoing. We also need to frequently check our hearts to make absolutely certain we're not grieving or quenching, and that we're asking for His power, patience, and boldness. The end result will be a transforming focus on heaven and a sensitivity to the opportunity and joy of being in the harvest.

> *When we grieve the Holy Spirit, we're doing what He says not to do. On the other hand, quenching the Spirit is not doing what He says to do.*

How to Be Filled With the Spirit

There is no strict, rigid system that tells us step-by-step how we can be filled with the Holy Spirit. If we want to understand how we can be filled with the Spirit, all we need to do is look at the book of Acts and what happened to the disciples. They give us some biblical examples that we can learn from and apply to our own lives.

Believe

We have to believe that we need the Holy Spirit. We have to believe that we can't do what God has called us to do on our own. We have to see from Jesus' and the early church's example that they needed Him and we need Him. We have to believe that He will continually fill us and enable us to keep our hearts in heaven and have our hands in the harvest.

Pray

It seems to me that the Holy Spirit responds to people who are prayerful and believing, as the disciples were in Acts 2 and 4. We repeatedly see that the Spirit falls as people pray.

Obey

We have to do whatever Jesus tells us to do. He told the disciples to go to Jerusalem; they went to Jerusalem. He didn't tell them how long to wait, but they waited ten days. Paul tells us that when we don't obey, we grieve the Holy Spirit, and then He pulls out of what we're trying to do. Obedience is critical to being filled with the Holy Spirit because He responds to it. Do what Jesus tells you in order to be filled with power!

Hunger

The first disciples waited and prayed for ten days—that is faith, obedience, and hunger! They were hungering for the Spirit of God to come and fulfill the promise of Jesus, the promise of the Father. I love what Jesus said in Luke 11:13: "If you then, being evil, know how to give good gifts to your children, how much more will your heavenly Father give the Holy Spirit to those who ask Him!" When we hunger for His Spirit, the Father gives us His Spirit.

Ask

Hungering and asking are linked—we just read that in Luke 11:13. Asking doesn't mean a nonchalant petition. *Asking* in the Greek means "to beg, to crave, to hunger." It's not that God is reluctant; it's that He wants to see if we're serious. He wants to know if we're really hungering for more of Him and His harvest.

Receive

We need to receive instead of quenching, limiting, restricting, and resisting, even if it begins to feel *a bit* supernatural. The disciples didn't resist the Holy Spirit. Even with the wind blowing and tongues of flames around them, they received what God gave them.

Labor

This Christian life isn't about lounging. It's interesting to me that those who were filled were going after God—they were serious about His harvest, and God filled them. God saw that they were a good investment. God saw that they were so serious about the Kingdom of God and the gospel of Jesus Christ that they were willing to labor.

Do you recognize your need for the Holy Spirit to come upon you with power in order for you to witness for Jesus? Or are you fine doing what you're doing on your own? Are you living your life in such a way that He has to fill you? Or do you have it all under control?

Remember, *your* control will produce *your* results, and they won't be very much.

When you believe, pray, obey, hunger, ask, receive, and labor, God will powerfully fill you with His Holy Spirit. Then you'll produce His results, which are eternal.

There's a huge difference between "not very much" and "eternal." Choose to be filled with the Spirit and watch what God can do in you and through you.

11

The Rewards of Heaven

Over the past nine chapters we've seen the tension in which we live, and we understand Paul's frustration—he was torn between two worlds. He was eager to be with Jesus and at the same time he had compassion for people's needs. He saw the plentiful harvest and he wanted to help broken, needy people find Jesus. He had a tug-of-war raging in him, and through it all, his heart was open and so were his hands.

There's an interesting paradox in Paul's life. The more he focused on Jesus and heaven, the more he was torn to stay here and be involved in the harvest. The more he knew the Person of Jesus Christ, the more he wanted to tell people about Him.

This concluding chapter reinforces the tension of being torn between heaven and remaining here on earth to serve others. It should serve as a launching pad for you as it encourages you to be hard-pressed—looking to heaven—while at the same time seeking earthly opportunities to reach out to others with the message of Jesus' love.

169

The Seriousness of Serving

Having your hand actively in the harvest is more important than you may have ever realized. Somewhere along the line you've probably been taught that being a Christian is saying the prayer, showing up in church, and being a little nicer than you used to be. Here's a shocker—that is not the ultimate goal.

The ultimate goal is being Jesus to whomever you find yourself next to—wherever it is, at whatever time, day or night, with everything you have—and someday to be with Jesus face-to-face. These two things should define our Christian lives. We live our lives with our hearts in heaven and our hands ready to reach other people. It's an old saying but so true: "Your actions are the only Bible some people are ever going to read." So, what are they reading when they look at us?

> *The ultimate goal is being Jesus to whomever you find yourself next to—wherever it is, at whatever time, day or night, with everything you have—and someday to be with Jesus face-to-face.*

Jesus gives us some help. In Matthew 24 and 25 He's speaking to His disciples near the end of His time on earth. These are in essence His parting words, and they are some of the most serious and sober words He's spoken. In this section of Scripture He tells four parables. He knows He is on His way to heaven and He leaves His team (and us) with a reminder of the importance of serving.

The Faithful Servant and the Evil Servant

The four parables start in Matthew 24:44–51 with a parable showing a contrast between a faithful and an evil servant.

The faithful servant is expectant. He has a hopeful expectation of Jesus' return. Because he lives expectantly, he lives righteously and does his best to do the will of God. He's a worker. He is a passionate servant of all that his Lord commands him to do.

He is rewarded. Jesus said, "I'm going to make you ruler over all My goods."

The evil servant, unlike the faithful servant, is totally unexpectant. Jesus' return isn't on his radar, and he lives accordingly. He treats other people horribly. He's about living for the *now*, not the eternal. The evil servant is also ignorant. He not only doesn't expect Jesus to return, he's spiritually clueless about what the Word says about Jesus' second coming.

Jesus says this servant will be cut in two and go to a place where there's weeping and gnashing of teeth. The evil servant is facing severe judgment and punishment.

Both are "rewarded" and both are called servants. The question we need to answer is what kind of servants are we? Are our hands open to serve, or are they closed? Are our hearts expectantly in heaven's eternity, or are we focused on the *now*?

Wise and Foolish Virgins

Matthew 25:1–13 gives us the second parable about being a servant.

We're introduced to five wise virgins. Just like the faithful servant in the first parable, these wise virgins were expectant. They were watching and waiting for the coming of the bridegroom.

They were also prepared. They had oil in both their lamps and their vessels (base-like plates or reservoirs) so that they could keep burning as long as it was necessary. Oil in the New Testament represents the Holy Spirit. Jesus is showing us that these wise virgins are like those filled with the Holy Spirit.

They were also informed. They knew they had to have their own oil. Nobody could get it for them—they had to ask and receive the anointing of the Holy Spirit themselves. They could not rely on anything or anyone but God.

Because they lived expectantly, waited patiently, worked to prepare, and sought the fullness of the Holy Spirit, the virgins were asked into the wedding when the bridegroom came.

The foolish virgins, on the other hand, were not prepared. They were not informed. They didn't realize they could not ride on other people's coattails. They didn't know the truth from the Word, so they wasted time and energy on foolish things instead of asking and receiving what God had for them.

The bridegroom told the foolish virgins, "I never knew you." They could be compared to "almost Christians." They were part of the group but not active in the body. In the end, they were left out.

The Parable of the Talents

Jesus goes on and tells a third parable in Matthew 25:14–30. This one goes even further in explaining how important serving in the harvest is to Jesus. Do you realize that one day there is going to be a settling of accounts? We'll talk about rewards in a few pages, but this parable shines a significant light on how accounts are settled.

The servants in this parable were workers. The five- and two-talent servants were wise because they took what their lord gave them and worked hard. They doubled what they were given.

Consequently, their lord rewarded them. When it was time for an accounting of what they had accomplished, he rewarded their efforts with more. He affirmed them and said, "Well done, good and faithful servant." Wow, wouldn't all of us like to hear those words from Jesus? It's possible when our hand is in the harvest, we're anointed with the Holy Spirit, and we're willing to do what He's called us to do.

Let's not get hung up on why God gave different talents to each servant. That's not important. God is sovereign and He can do whatever He wants to do. What is important is that these two servants took what was given to them by the grace of God and said, "After all my Master has done for me, I'm going to do something for Him." They worked wisely, multiplied what was given them, and were rewarded.

The one-talent servant had a much different attitude. He was completely clueless about the very character and nature of God. He was also unthankful, bitter, rebellious, and prideful. He was an excuse maker. Jesus called him an "unprofitable servant." He was cast into outer darkness.

Two servants are rewarded and affirmed, the other one is cast into darkness. Do you see Jesus' point? Having our hand in the harvest and serving people with what He's given us is extremely important. It's what we need to be doing as Christians, and we get the right attitude by having our hearts in heaven.

Sheep and Goats

The last parable in this set is found in Matthew 25:31–46.

The people represented as sheep served the last, the least, and the lost. Because of their faithfulness Jesus said to them, "Come, you blessed of My Father, you have an inheritance awaiting you that was being prepared for you before the foundation of the world—for eternal life in heaven" (v. 34, my paraphrase).

Their hearts were was in heaven and their hands were in the harvest. They loved God and they loved people, and their love for people manifested itself in serving others. They felt the love of God so strongly that they had to show it to other people; by doing that, they were actually serving Jesus.

The people represented as goats were in trouble. Jesus asked them to depart from Him. They rejected serving other people and serving God, and their "reward" was to be taken away from Jesus. Devastating.

They lived selfishly, they were clueless to the needs around them, and they were so focused on themselves that they received eternal separation from God.

Remember in chapter 8 we talked about mistaken priorities and responsible excuses? The goats are perfect examples of both.

These four parables show us Jesus' priorities. He wants us torn between two worlds, hard-pressed between heaven and earth. He wants our hearts to be in heaven and our hands to be in the harvest, and all He's asking us to do is study the Word, be filled with the Holy Spirit's power, live expectantly, reach out to others, and meet needs.

Rewarded for Our Deeds

In an earlier chapter I quoted Paul's writing in 1 Corinthians 3:10–15. At that point I stressed that Paul was carefully calculating a foundation that keeps his heart in heaven and his hand in the harvest.

This Scripture also gives us a picture of our reward in heaven. In the first part of his statement Paul tells us that God is entrusting work to us (vv. 10–12). Then it is to be tested by Him (vv. 13–15). We're given work to do by God, and that work will either be something of eternal value or not. Enduring work receives a reward. Work that is burned will be a loss and the person will suffer a loss of reward.

There will be a final accounting, and how we serve (whether we're like the wise servants and the sheep, or the foolish servants and the goats) will determine our rewards in heaven.

We can't miss one of Paul's important points. Remember he's torn between two worlds. In this passage He shows us that the very Christ whom we serve here is the One before whom we shall stand in judgment. It's important to know that everything that will eventually be known will not strike fear in the hearts of those who have discovered His love and forgiveness. It's also important to keep in mind that we won't fear this moment of standing before Jesus if we've had our hands in the harvest.

We're given work to do by God, and that work will either be something of eternal value or not.

Do you think the guys with two and five talents were worried when the time for an accounting came? Do you think the wise virgins were worried when the bridegroom showed up? Do you think the sheep were distressed? No way! They had nothing to fear because they were exactly like Paul—torn between two worlds with their hearts in heaven and their hands in the harvest. I quoted this verse in an earlier chapter, but it's good to remember the advice Jesus gives us in Matthew 6:20: "Lay up for yourselves treasures in heaven, where neither moth nor rust destroys and where thieves do not break in and steal." He's talking about eternal rewards. He's telling us that while we're here on this earth, we need to lay up treasures in heaven that won't ever be destroyed. Every person we serve, everyone with whom we share Jesus, and every moment we spend praying with someone whose life is broken and twisted by this crazy world is a treasure in heaven. It's part of our reward and it comes from having an open heart to heaven and an open hand to people here on this earth. Paul knew it, Jesus taught it, and we just need to do it!

Promises of Heaven

The best motivation for putting our hands in the harvest is to fully understand the heaven of the Bible and heaven's promises. We've talked a lot about heaven, but let me give you some concrete promises about it from God. These are promises that you can trust in and completely rely upon. Understanding these promises will help get you started. They will give you concrete footing so that when you move out to serve and put your hands in the harvest, you'll have these heavenly promises as your spiritual support. This isn't an exhaustive list. I'd challenge you to find your own as you read your Bible more and come to see all that heaven is.

God Promises a Home

In John 14:2, Jesus tells us that in His Father's house there are many mansions. If you are a believer, one of these will be yours! Revelation 21:1 tells us that our current home, this earth, is passing away. Revelation 21:2 gives us a glimpse of the New Jerusalem. The apostle John tells us more in Revelation 21:9–21.

God Promises Himself

Jeremiah 31:33 and Ezekiel 37:26–28 make it clear that God wants to be among us. Revelation 21:3 fulfills those promises as He shows us His presence as never before. God Himself will dwell with us forever.

God Promises Happiness

Revelation 21:4 tells us that God will wipe away every tear; there shall be no more death, sorrow, or crying. Pain and suffering will be gone eternally.

God Promises Hope

Revelation 21:5–6 says,

> He who sat on the throne said, "Behold, I make all things new." And He said to me, "Write, for these words are true and faithful." And He said to me, "It is done! I am the Alpha and the Omega, the Beginning and the End. I will give of the fountain of the water of life freely to him who thirsts."

Our hope is based on His absolute guarantee—these words are true and faithful—and if we have any questions, we can look at His absolute greatness as the Alpha and the Omega.

We can firmly stand on these heavenly promises. As our hearts look to heaven, we have these promises as an anchor for our souls. Stand firm, have your heart in heaven and your hand in the harvest.

Paul wrote in Colossians 1:4–5, "We have heard of your faith in Christ Jesus and your love for all of God's people, which come from your confident hope of what God has reserved for you in heaven" (NLT). God's promises of heaven are reserved for you. They are set aside just for you. They give you hope, and that hope causes you to reach out in love for all of God's people. It's a calling based on His reserved promises.

Faith in Action

James 2:17–18 says, "Faith by itself, if it does not have works, is dead. But someone will say, 'You have faith, and I have works.' Show me your faith without your works, and I will show you my faith by my works.'"

It doesn't get more graphic than this statement—faith by itself, without accompanying works, is dead. James had a legitimate concern about the early church, and it's just as much a concern today. R. Kent Hughes wrote,

> It was just as likely then as today for church attenders to slide along with a bogus faith that made no real difference in the way they lived. James wants to make crystal-clear what makes faith real faith, and in doing so he sheds eternal wisdom on the relationship of faith and action.[1]

Paul, handcuffed in a disgusting cell, ankle deep in wastewater, witnessed to his jailer. Faith in action.

Stephen, facing a stoning and certain death, spoke clearly about Jesus to his accusers. Faith in action.

Peter, a fisherman, knew God's Word and preached it despite criticism and jail. Faith in action.

A million years from now, you'll still be glad you had your heart in heaven and your hand in the harvest.

Rahab, a harlot, trusted the Lord and saved Jewish soldiers. Faith in action.

The list goes on and on.

As we look at our lives today, we have to ask, "What kind of Christian do I want to be?" Are we willing to commit firmly to having our hearts in heaven, getting into His Word, and letting the Holy Spirit guide and lead us into the plentiful harvest? Are we willing to see the need, have compassion, and meet it?

Are you willing to live as a wise servant and not a foolish one?

Here's the good news. You can make a decision to live a "profitable" life for Jesus right now.

With God's help and your heart firmly set on heaven's home, healing, and hope, you can do it. You can live torn between heaven and earth as Paul did. You can compassionately see the harvest and you can fill the shortage of labor with your hands. You'll discover the joy of heaven, the joy of serving others, and the joy of seeing other people receive Jesus as their Lord and Savior.

A million years from now, you'll still be glad you had your heart in heaven and your hand in the harvest.

Bible Study Resources

Resource	Description
Study Bible	We recommend the *NKJV Study Bible*. This is Pastor Steve's favored translation, and this is one of the most comprehensive study Bibles available. It includes commentary, charts, graphs, etc., to help you study and know God's Word.
Bible Dictionary	We recommend the *Nelson Illustrated Bible Dictionary* or *Unger's Bible Dictionary*. You can better understand the Bible with definitions explaining Bible terms and information on people, places, culture, and history.
Bible Handbook	We recommend *Halley's Bible Handbook*, an at-a-glance and book-by-book survey of every book of the Bible addressing "who, what, where, when, and why." We also recommend *What the Bible Is All About* by Henrietta Mears. You will find essential facts and historical background, but more important see how every book of the Bible points to Jesus and God's plan to transform everyone's life through faith in Him.
Concordance	We recommend *Strong's Concordance*. You can find every word in the Bible each place it occurs and find relevant passages easily. It also gives the Greek and Hebrew meanings of each word.

In Defense of the Faith	We recommend *Kingdom of the Cults* by Walter Martin, a comprehensive resource on cult religions and how to biblically defend yourself from them. We also recommend *77 FAQs About God and the Bible* by Josh McDowell. It offers concise, accessible presentations when readers want an apologetic reference or need to answer a question about their faith.
Computer Software	We recommend e-Sword. This comprehensive software is free to download from: http://e-sword.net.

Notes

Chapter 1: A Renewed Heavenly Vision

1. Billy Graham, *Death and the Life After* (Nashville: W Publishing Group, 1987), 175.

2. Dee Brestin, *A Woman of Contentment: Ecclesiastes* (Colorado Springs: David C. Cook, 2006), 20.

3. William Barclay, *The Letters to the Philippians, Colossians, and Thessalonians* (Louisville, KY: Westminster John Knox Press, 1975, 2003), 33–34.

Chapter 2: A Passion for Hard-Pressed Living

1. Charles R. Swindoll, *Paul: A Man of Grace and Grit* (Nashville: Thomas Nelson, 2002), 22.

2. F. F. Bruce, *The Epistle to the Galatians: A Commentary on the Greek Text* (Grand Rapids: Wm. B. Eerdmans Publishing, 1982), 89.

3. Witness Lee, *Life Study of Galatians: Messages 1–24* (Anaheim, CA: Living Stream Ministry, 1984), 92.

4. Henry Blackaby, *Created to Be God's Friend: How God Shapes Those He Loves* (Nashville: Thomas Nelson, 1999), ebook edition.

5. The judgment seat (*bema*) was a raised platform (sometimes portable) that could be reached by steps. It was a place where orations were made. Rulers used the *bema* to elevate them above a trial so they could observe, hear testimonies, and dole out judgments. Scripture speaks of the *bema* twice in reference to the divine tribunal before which believers will stand (Romans 14:10; 2 Corinthians 5:10). (See M. G. Easton, *Easton's Bible Dictionary,* Public Domain, Logos Electronic Version.)

6. Randy Alcorn, *The Light of Eternity: Perspectives on Heaven* (Colorado Springs: WaterBrook Press, 1999), 135.

7. General William Booth, *General Booth's Vision and Other Addresses* (New York: Pickett Publishing Co., 1903), 26.

8. Warren Wiersbe, *Ten People Every Christian Should Know* (Grand Rapids, Baker Books: 2011), ebook edition.

9. Henry and Norman Blackaby, *Called & Accountable 52-Week Devotional: Discovering Your Place in God's Eternal Purpose* (Birmingham, AL: New Hope Publishers, 2007), 39.

10. John MacArthur, *Colossians: The MacArthur New Testament Commentary* (Chicago: Moody Press, 1992), Logos electronic version.

11. Mike Tucker, *Meeting Jesus in the Book of Revelation* (Nampa, ID: Pacific Press Publishing Association, 2007), 44.

12. Spiros Zodhiates, *The Complete Word Study Dictionary: New Testament* (Chattanooga, TN: AMG Publishers, 1992), e-Sword electronic edition.

13. Ibid.

14. Ibid.

15. Ted Dekker, *The Slumber of Christianity: Awakening a Passion for Heaven on Earth*, (Nashville: Thomas Nelson, Inc., 2005), ebook edition.

Chapter 3: Heaven Is Our Real Home

1. Max Lucado, *The Great House of God: A Home for Your Heart* (Nashville: Thomas Nelson, 1997), 3.

2. C. S. Lewis, *Mere Christianity* in *The Complete C. S. Lewis Signature Classics* (New York: HarperCollins, 2002), 114.

3. Mother Teresa (compiled by Lucinda Vardey), *A Simple Path* (New York: Random House, 1995), 73.

4. Spiros Zodhiates, *The Complete Word Study Dictionary: New Testament,* e-Sword edition.

5. Ibid.

6. Jonathan Edmondson, *Scripture Views of the Heavenly World* (New York: G. Lane & C. B. Tippett, 1846), ebook edition.

7. Augustus William Hare, *Sermons to a Country Congregation, Second Volume* (London: J. Hatchard and Son, 1836), 202.

8. Zodhiates, *The Complete Word Study Dictionary: New Testament.*

9. Randy Alcorn, *Heaven* (Carol Stream, IL: Tyndale House Publishers, 2004), 20.

Chapter 4: Heaven Is Our Real Hope

1. E. M. Bounds, *Heaven: A City, A Home* (London: Oliphants, Ltd., and Fleming H. Revell Company, 1921), 145.

2. Spiros Zodhiates, *The Complete Word Study Dictionary: New Testament.*

3. Ibid.

4. Ibid.

5. Jonathan Edmondson, *Scripture Views of the Heavenly World* (New York: G. Lane & C. B. Tippett, 1846), ebook edition.

6. Spiros Zodhiates, *The Complete Word Study Dictionary: New Testament.*

7. Robert Hall and John Foster, *The Works of Rev. John Hall, A.M.* (New York: J. & J. Harper, 1833), 328.

8. Jonathan Edmondson, *Scripture Views of the Heavenly World* (New York: G. Lane & C. B. Tippett, 1846), ebook edition.

9. C. S. Lewis, *The Dark Tower & Other Stories* (New York: Harcourt Brace Jovanovich, 1977), 49.

Chapter 5: A Glimpse of Heaven

1. Rebecca Ruter Springer, *My Dream of Heaven* (Tulsa, OK: Harrison House, 2002, originally titled *Intra Muros*, 1898), 8.

2. F. F. Bruce, *The Epistles to the Colossians, to Philemon, and to the Ephesians* (Grand Rapids: Wm. B. Eerdmans Publishing Co, 1984), 131.

3. John Eldredge, *The Journey of Desire* (Nashville: Thomas Nelson, 2000), 111.

4. Randy Alcorn, *Heaven*, 407.

5. Mark Buchanan, *Things Unseen: Living with Eternity in Your Heart* (Sisters, OR: Multnomah, 2002), ebook edition.

Chapter 6: What Will We Do in Heaven?

1. Michael D. C. Drout, ed., *J. R. R. Tolkien Encyclopedia: Scholarship and Critical Assessment* (New York: Routledge, Taylor & Francis Group, 2007), 267.

2. Alcorn, *Heaven*, 397.

3. Rev. T. M. Morris, "An Old and a New Song," in *The Baptist Magazine* (London: Yates and Alexander, 1880).

4. Leland Ryken, James C. Wilhoit, and Tremper Longman, *The Dictionary of Biblical Imagery* (Downers Grove, IL: InterVarsity Press, 1998), 52.

5. Colleen McDannell and Berhnard Lang, *Heaven: A History* (New Haven, CT: Yale University Press, 1988), 47.

6. Liz Curtis Higgs, *Help! I'm Laughing and I Can't Get Up* (Nashville: Thomas Nelson, 1998), ebook edition.

7. Walter Hooper, editor, *The Business of Heaven: Daily Readings from C. S. Lewis* (New York: Harcourt, 1984), ebook edition.

8. Bill Adler, *Ask Billy Graham: The World's Most Beloved Preacher Answers Your Most Important Questions* (Nashville: Thomas Nelson, 2007), 216. (Note: The quote was originally published in the *Philadelphia Inquirer*, February 7, 1999.)

9. St. Augustine, *The City of God*, translated by Marcus Dods, D.D. (Peabody, MA: Hendrickson Publishers, 2009), 779.

10. Charles H. Spurgeon, *The Treasury of David* (Grand Rapids: Kregel Publications, 1968, 1976), ebook edition.

Chapter 7: Heaven Is for Healing

1. Randy Alcorn, *Heaven*, 240.

2. H. Wayne House & William Grover, *Does God Feel Your Pain? Finding Answers When Life Hurts* (Eugene, OR: Harvest House Publishers, 2009), 42.

3. Warren W. Wiersbe, *The Wiersbe Bible Commentary: New Testament* (Colorado Springs: David C. Cook, 2007), 514.

Chapter 8: Having Our Hands in the Harvest

1. John R. W. Stott, *Christian Mission in the Modern World* (Downers Grove, IL: InterVarsity Press, 1975), 21.

2. Mike Barnett, *Discovering the Mission of God: Missional Practices for the 21st Century* (Downers Grove, IL: InterVarsity Press, 2012), 19.

3. Darrell L. Bock, *The NIV Application Commentary: Luke* (Grand Rapids: Zondervan, 1996), cclxxxiv.

4. C. H. Spurgeon, *The Devotional Classics of C. H. Spurgeon, Morning & Evening I & II* (Lafayette, IN: Sovereign Grace Publishers, 1990), 26.

5. David McGee, *Cross the Bridge Every Day* (Xulon Press, 2011), 113.

Chapter 9: The Power of Knowing God's Word

1. *Mercer Dictionary of the Bible* says, "After the martyrdom of Stephen, he [Philip] left Jerusalem and fled to Samaria where he started a successful mission later sanctioned by the apostles in Jerusalem (Acts 8:14). Simon Magus is said to have been one of his converts (8:13). Two decades after the beginning of the mission to the gentiles Paul was a guest in the home of Philip, and his four daughters who had the gift of prophecy." *Mercer Dictionary of the Bible*, Watson E. Mills General Editor (Macon, GA: Mercer University Press, 1990), 682.

2. David Van Biema, "The Case for Teaching the Bible," *Time*, March 22, 2007.

3. Collin Hansen, "Why Johnny Can't Read the Bible," *Christianity Today*, May 2010.

4. Alec Gallup and Wendy W. Simmons, "Six in Ten Americans Read Bible at Least Occasionally," The Gallup Organization, October 20, 2000, www.gallup.com/poll/2416/Six-Ten-Americans-Read-Bible-Least-Occasionally.aspx.

5. "Barna Studies the Research, Offers a Year-In-Review Perspective," Barna Group, December 18, 2009, https://www.barna.org/barna-update/article/12-faith spirituality/325-barna-studies-the-research-offers-a-year-in-review-perspective.

6. "Bible Literacy Project News," *Chicago Tribune*, May 12, 2005.

7. Collin Hansen, "Why Johnny Can't Read the Bible."

8. Spiros Zodhiates, *The Complete Word Study Dictionary: New Testament*, e-Sword Edition.

9. Warren W. Wiersbe, *The Wiersbe Bible Commentary: The Complete New Testament* (Colorado Springs: David C. Cook Publishing, 2007), 782.

10. R. C. Sproul, *Knowing Scripture* (Downers Grove, IL: InterVarsity Press, 2009), 25.

11. John Piper, *What Jesus Demands from the World* (Wheaton, IL: Crossway Books, 2006), 65.

12. R. A. Torrey, *The Importance and Value of Proper Bible Study* (Chicago: Moody Press, 1921), 23.

Chapter 10: The Power of the Holy Spirit

1. "Christians Say They Do Best at Relationships, Worst in Bible Knowledge," The Barna Group, June 14, 2005, www.barna.org/barna-update/article/

5-barna-update/177-christians-say-they-do-best-at-relationships-worst-in-bible-knowledge#.UjIVpqzhd8E.

Chapter 11: The Rewards of Heaven

1. R. Kent Hughes, *James: Faith That Works* (Wheaton, IL: Crossway Books, 1991), 108.

Steve Berger is the senior pastor to more than four thousand people at Grace Chapel, Leipers Fork, Tennessee. Steve is also a part of the teaching faculty for the National Worship Leader Conference and regularly contributes to several publications. Steve is the author of *40 Days With the Word of Promise DVD* and *Participant's Guide* (Thomas Nelson, 2008), and *Have Heart*, coauthored with Sarah Berger.